D1616976

A GUIDE TO TREASURE IN

ARIZONA

By Thomas Penfield

Cover Illustration by Eugene Shortridge

TRUE TREASURE LIBRARY

Other books available from True Treasure Library —

- DIRECTORY OF BURIED OR SUNKEN TREASURES AND LOST MINES OF THE UNITED STATES
- TREASURE GUIDE TO NEBRASKA — KANSAS — NORTH DAKOTA — SOUTH DAKOTA
- A GUIDE TO TREASURE IN CALIFORNIA
- A GUIDE TO TREASURE IN TEXAS
- A GUIDE TO TREASURE IN ARKANSAS — LOUISIANA — MISSISSIPPI
- A GUIDE TO TREASURE IN ARIZONA
- A GUIDE TO TREASURE IN NEVADA
- A GUIDE TO TREASURE IN NEW MEXICO
- A GUIDE TO TREASURE IN MISSOURI
- A GUIDE TO TREASURE IN UTAH
- A GUIDE TO TREASURE IN ILLINOIS AND INDIANA
- A GUIDE TO TREASURE IN MICHIGAN AND OHIO
- A GUIDE TO TREASURE IN PENNSYLVANIA
- A GUIDE TO TREASURE IN VIRGINIA AND WEST VIRGINIA
- A GUIDE TO TREASURE IN KENTUCKY

ISBN 0941620-01-8

FREE Treasure Reference Catalog.   **Dealer Discounts available.**

reprinted and distributed by
CARSON ENTERPRISES
Drawer 71, Deming, NM 88031-0071

© **1973 by True Treasure Publications, Inc.**

TREASURE GUIDE SERIES

INTRODUCTION

The search for gold—and treasure—has been going on in Arizona since the first white men came to the region. In 1539 Fray Marcos de Niza was sent from Mexico to check reports of large cities and much wealth in precious metals and stones in the land to the north. He returned with glowing accounts of the Seven Cities of Cibola. What he saw, and only from a distance, were the Zuni pueblas of Hawikuh, but his story was enough to attract a horde of other treasure seekers to the land, notably Francisco Vasquez de Coronado.

Following in the footsteps of the swashbuckling conquistadores, Jesuit priests entered Arizona, introducing to the natives such modern amenities as cattle, housing and cultivated crops along with religion. In return, the friendly natives showed the padres where there were rich deposits of gold and silver. With the help of their Indian neophytes, these precious metals were mined by the padres and brought to camps and missions to be hidden away for safekeeping until they could be transported to Mexico and hence to Spain.

But not all of the Indian tribes in Arizona were friendly. This was especially true of the Apaches, who fiercely resented the white man's intrusion upon their lands. Many of the mining camps and missions were attacked by the Apaches, who frequently killed all occupants and destroyed both campsite and mission site. Such was the case of the Escalante Mine, the famous "Mine With the Iron Door." It was discovered by Indians in 1689 and worked for many years by Father Escalante's charges. When Apaches attacked the camp and annihilated its workers, they obliterated all traces of the mine and the camp. Neither have been found to this day. Repeated over and over, these acts left Arizona with an intriguing and confusing legacy of lost mission treasures and lost mines.

When Americans started the push westward with the news of the discovery of gold in California, tens of thousands of them rushed across Arizona, completely unaware of the vast mineral wealth under their feet. When this great wealth was finally tapped, mining and milling camps in untold numbers sprang up in Arizona wherever precious metals were found. Some of these grew into permanent settlements, but for the most part, when the ores were exhausted, their occupants simply walked away and left the towns to slip into oblivion as ghosts. While many of the more publicized and easily reached of these ghost towns have been rather thoroughly explored by treasure and relic hunters, others are tucked away in remote mountain canyons, safe from the ravages of vandals and unfamiliar to the click of metal detectors.

Arizona also had more than its share of blood-and-thunder days—the stuff of which treasure legends are born. Hostile Indians raided its ranches and mining camps, carrying away and concealing treasures they had little use for but wanted to deny the white man. Outlaws preyed upon the bullion trains packing gold and silver from the mines, ambushed stages carrying Wells

Fargo chests, and held up passenger trains as they stopped for water at lonely tank stations. Much of the treasure seized by these bandits was cached for recovery at a later date that, for one reason or another, never arrived.

The reader of this volume will note a startling similarity between certain stories, seemingly with only the names of people and places being different. Doubtless some of these are one and the same story, but in an anthology such as this completeness is the goal rather than sorting facts from legend. And who, in the final analysis, is there to say with positive authority that this story is true and that version false? In most cases, too much time has elapsed and the final authorities are all dead.

The highway numbers used herein are also those found in the Rand McNally Road Atlas, but it should be pointed out that these assigned numbers are sometimes changed, especially as interstate highway numbers replace state or county numbers. Remember also that portions of highways are frequently relocated, and that new highways come into being from time to time.

A special word of warning is given here to those treasure hunters and lost mine and artifact seekers who are not familiar with Arizona's desert sections, which cover a vast area of the southwestern quarter of the state. Excessive heat, coupled with a scarcity of water, make these desert regions dangerous for off-road travel by the uninitiated during much of the year— and regions requiring for cautious travel at any time.

A further word of warning is directed to those making searches in areas of open shaft mining. In many sections of the state, the terrain is still pocked with hundreds of open shafts—some descending to amazing depths. When these become covered with broken branches and shrubbery, they can be veritable death traps for the unwary.

Archaeologically, the State of Arizona has few rivals in the scope of its sites, but strict laws regulate the gathering and disposition of artifacts of any kind. It is recommended that you familiarize yourself with Arizona's Antiquarian Act if you are interested in such activity.

Good luck and good hunting!

Thomas Penfield
Los Angeles, California
May, 1973

ARIZONA

TREASURE SITES

Apache County—In 1875 Jim Carson and a Mexican helper were engaged in operating a small freighting business between Fort Defiance, almost on the New Mexico line in northeastern Arizona, and Camp Verde, on the Verde River in Yavapai County. The two men made camp one night on the Pueblo Colorado Wash near the vicinity of what is now the Indian village of Ganado on the Navajo Indian Reservation. In the morning one of the mules was missing, and while the Mexican moved on with the rest of the train, Carson went in search of the animal, believing that it would be found grazing nearby and he could easily catch up with the train.

As he had suspected, the mule was located less than a mile away. Retracing his steps to the campsite with the animal, Carson's attention was drawn to what he thought was an unusual mineral formation—a bed of glistening black sand—in a wash. Investigation revealed that the sand contained flecks of gold, and digging down, Carson found that he could pick out nuggets of pure gold. It was plain to see that the bed of sand stretched over a large area. Nearby was a small spring. Carson erected a small pole to mark the spot, pocketed some of the nuggets, and hastened to rejoin his partner.

Wisely keeping the news to himself, Carson returned alone to the site the following spring and took out $2,500 worth of gold. But realizing he would have to have help if he was to take out any great quantity of the gold, he returned to Fort Defiance determined to find a partner. An agreement was reached with Jack Williams, a trader living near the fort. Williams was to go to the placer and build a cabin while Carson went to California to get his brother.

But Williams was unable to locate the site from Carson's description and returned to Fort Defiance to await his return. Months went by and Carson did not show up. About a year later Williams learned that Carson had been killed by Indians. Williams organized an expedition and searched a wide area around Pueblo Colorado Wash, but without success. It was concluded that Indians had found the evidence of Carson's mining, pulled up the marker pole, and covered every trace of the ore-bearing black sand.

ARIZONA

Apache County—The Cibecue Apaches had gold and knew its trading value—a fact well known to the pioneers who had occasion to barter with them. Old Chief Al-che-sa's people roamed the White Mountain country under more contented circumstances than most Arizona tribes enjoyed. Chief Al-che-sa had gained some degree of fame as a scout for the army, and as the mediator at Geronimo's surrender to General Crook in 1886.

Al-che-sa was friendly and on good terms with the white settlers, but the members of his clan were sullen and dangerous if permitted to be so by their leader. Jealously guarding their portion of the San Carlos Reservation, which ran along Cibecue Creek in the northeastern corner of Apache county, they did not permit white men to roam there without tribal permission— and it was seldom granted.

According to popular belief at the time, the reason why white men were not welcome in the domain of the Cibecue Apaches was that they had a placer field of gold of great richness hidden away in the mountain fastness of their guarded lands. Al-che-sa himself, it is said, always had plenty of gold nuggets on his person and traded them generously in the surrounding white settlements. On one occasion he offered a nugget worth $500 for $10 worth of supplies.

The Cibecues only laughed when asked about the source of their gold. Prospectors who left with announced intentions of going into the Cibecue country were often never heard of again. Many thought they approached too close to the hidden placer and were killed by the Apache guards.

Many old prospectors had a theory that Al-che-sa's mine was actually the Lost Adams Diggings, which is generally placed in northwestern New Mexico not too far distant from the San Carlos Reservation. **Map Code 8 D-5**

Apache County—There are two well-known lost mine stories bearing the name Lost Adams, one placed in Arizona, the other in New Mexico, and the name Adams figures in several other stories of lost mines in the Southwest. Because the Lost Adams Diggings story based in New Mexico had its origin in Arizona, it is often confused with the Lost Adams Mine of Arizona, sometimes called the "Lost Adams Cave."

Shortly after the Navajo Indians had been confined to their reservation along the northern New Mexico-Arizona border, and soldiers were stationed to keep them there, a man named Henry Adams (some accounts say it was Jim Adams) established a small trading post at Fort Defiance, Arizona. There is still a small town there by this name.

Adams catered to the Indians and few white men ever patronized his store. The Indians learned to respect Adams and they were as friendly as their injured pride would permit them to be. Adams minded his own business, got along with the military, and didn't force himself on the Indians.

One day three young Indians came to the store and made extensive selections of merchandise, helping themselves from the shelves, as was their custom. When they were ready to go, one of the Indians dumped the contents

7

of a buckskin bag on the counter. Chattering among themselves, they picked up their merchandise and stalked out. The contents of the bag were gold nuggets —more than enough to pay for their purchases. Adams knew the Indians were that way with their gold, and he guessed that the gold came from the hills on the reservation. He also determined to find out just where its source was located.

Slowly, discreetly, Adams set out to make friends of the three Indian bucks. They could not be pushed and he had to be extremely careful about showing any interest in their gold lest they become suspicious. After many more visits to the trading post, the three Indians gradually loosened up and talked. When Adams first mentioned the subject of gold, the Indians froze up immediately. Still, Adams did not give up. Over a period of time he did many little things for the Indians that eventually won their complete confidence. Gradually they came to the point of discussing the gold with Adams, and many visits later they agreed to take him to its source.

Leaving the post at night, the four men rode until early daybreak when they stopped at the mouth of a canyon. Here Adams was asked to submit to a blindfold. The horses were tethered and the Indians led the white man up a rough trail along the canyon wall. Finally they entered the mouth of a cave and Adams felt a rush of cool air that led him to believe that the cave had a second entrance. They traveled through a narrow passage to a large room. Here they halted and the blindfold was removed from Adams' eyes. What he saw struck him dumb with amazement. The floor of the cavernous room was literally covered with gold nuggets and ingots!

Adams was given no more than a quick look and the blindfold was again applied. He requested permission to carry away some of the wealth, but his guides refused. On the journey down the canyon wall, Adams managed to slip the blindfold down and caught a fleeting glimpse of three peaks, alike in shape and standing in the form of a triangle. One of the Indians caught him in the act and he was allowed to see no more. The remainder of the ride to Fort Defiance was made in sullen silence as the Indians felt that Adams had betrayed them.

Adams could not forget the sight of the gold he had seen in the cave. As soon as he could do so he sold his stock of merchandise and thereafter spent all his time and small fortune searching for the Navajo treasure cave. Every effort failed. Every trail followed led laboriously to nothing. When he was finally broken in spirits and his funds were exhausted, he found his health failing. He went to Tucson where he told his story to Judge Griscom and the knowledge of the fantastic treasure cave reached the public, creating a wave of excitement. Financed by Griscom, Adams returned to the Navajo country and renewed his search for the cave. When his presence was discovered by the Indians he was wounded and driven out. Judge Griscom advanced more money and the search continued for three more years.

When Judge Griscom refused to finance additional searches, Adams secured help from other sources and led several expeditions into the Navajo country, each ending in dejected failure. Unable to raise further funds in Tucson, Adams decided to appeal to an old friend in Phoenix, but just before he boarded the stage he learned of the man's death. Nevertheless, Adams left on the Phoenix stage. Just outside Tucson, the driver heard a shot and looking down, saw the form of a man topple from the open door. Henry Adams, failing to find the Navajo treasure cave, had placed a gun to his head and taken his own life.

Adams said the cave was located one day's ride out of Fort Defiance. That could have placed it in New Mexico, depending upon which directions the Indians had taken Adams. He apparently had no idea.

Cochise County—When Leonard Alvorsen, a one-time member of the Black Jack Ketchum gang of outlaws, was serving time in the Territorial Prison at Yuma, Arizona, he succeeded in passing information out to friends that the gang had buried treasure in one of their hideouts in the Chiricahua Mountains—a cave the gang called "Room Forty-four." These confidants, Bert and Harry Macia, searched the area without results.

When Black Jack himself was in jail after an abortive attempt to rob a train on Twin Mountain Curve in New Mexico, he told essentially the same story to Sheriff Cicero Stewart. Black Jack knew that he was going to be hanged—if he did not die of gangrene from an amputated arm as the result of a wound suffered in the attempted holdup. Later Black Jack told a cellmate that the story was a hoax intended to lead the sheriff into a trap in which he would be killed.

Accompanied by Sheriff Steve Roup of Bisbee, Stewart made a thorough search of the outlaw hideout near the old William Lutley ranch in Wildcat Canyon. The surviving members of the gang were not there to kill Stewart, and he did not find the supposed treasure. It is still believed that the Ketchum gang's treasure is unfound and repeated searches are still made for it.

Cochise County—Unlike most Apache chiefs of his time, Cochise did not molest Americans until he felt that he had been wronged by them. In 1880 he was accused of leading a raid on a ranch in his domain. Although he vehemently denied that he had taken any part in the raid, he was taken into custody by a tactless army officer who, among other things, accused him of being a liar. To a proud Indian like Cochise, this was the lowest of insults. From that day on he swore to fight a relentless war against all whites.

Cochise managed to escape almost immediately, and from then on until he practically dictated his own peace terms in 1882, he fought the U. S. Army to a standoff, raided emigrant trains and ranches and robbed stagecoaches. After stage operator Tom Jeffords had 28 of his men killed by Cochise's band in 16 months, he decided that something would have to be done if he was to remain in business. One day he rode alone into the Apache hideout in the Dragoon Mountains. He hardly expected to come out alive, but the old chief so admired the courage of "Red Whiskers," as the Indians knew Jeffords, that he not only spared Jefford's life but made him a blood brother. Thereafter, Jefford's stages were never bothered by Cochise's band.

But the old warrior had no such respect for the Butterfield stages that crossed his lands. Although he had no particular use for gold in the manner that the white man used it, he seized it from the Butterfield stages whenever possible. On one occasion he made off with two heavy iron chests filled with gold coins. Somehow his people managed to haul or drag the chests to the Apache hideout, known later as Cochise Stronghold in Stronghold Canyon in the rugged Dragoons where not even a horse could travel.

For years after Cochise's band made peace with white men—a peace made possible by Tom Jeffords—his people boasted that no white man would ever find the hidden chests of gold. Apparently the Indians were right. It is not known that they have ever been found.

Cochise County—When a young man known only as Simmons hired out to two brothers to cook and wrangle horses on a ranch about 30 miles northwest of Douglas, he assumed that they were legitimate ranchers. Soon he learned through overheard conversations that the brothers were really outlaws, and that they were planning to rob a large shipment of gold. Simmons asked to be taken in on the job, and after considerable consultation his request was granted.

During the successful robbery, Simmons was injured and lost the sight of an eye. Angered over his amateurish performance, one of the robbers wanted to kill him on the spot, but the other intervened and saved his life. Back at their camp, the two brothers took the two heavy bags of gold secured in the holdup and disappeared into the brush. When they returned empty-handed, Simmons protested that he should have his cut or know where the gold was hidden. He was told that he would know in time.

After a brief rest the three men rode south into Mexico, leaving the treasure behind lest they should be picked up and questioned about the robbery. Here Simmons was told bluntly that his services were no longer required. Fearing for his life, Simmons left at once, but he was afraid to return to Arizona and try to recover the treasure. He learned later that the two brothers had crossed the border into Arizona, where they had almost immediately been caught, charged with the crime and jailed.

Soon thereafter Simmons lost the sight of his other eye. Completely blind now, he lost all interest in the hidden gold. He did, however, tell two Americans who had befriended him where he thought the gold was concealed, but their search for the treasure failed. One could presume that the two outlaw brothers recovered the gold after their release from prison, but this has been denied. It may still be there.

Cochise County—A sign on the outskirts of Apache, Arizona (US 80), reads: "Skeleton Canyon 8 Miles." The wild stretches of the canyon wind into the Peloncillo Mountains and crosses the border into New Mexico. Through this canyon passed the old Smuggler's Trail from Sonora to Tucson, a route over which goods stolen in Mexico were transported to be sold in Arizona. And it was in this canyon that American outlaws waylaid the smuggling trains to steal their riches.

These outlaws were largely made up of gangs that hung out in Charleston and Galeyville where law and order were things unknown. Out of these wild and reckless towns—now both ghosts whose lurid pasts have all but been forgotten—the outlaws made periodic raids into Sonora, returning to Arizona to squander their riches in Cochise County honky-tonks. It was on one of these raids in 1881 that Curly Bill Brocius and his henchmen learned of an unusually rich train that was soon to pass through Skeleton Canyon. Plans were made immediately to intercept it.

When spies brought word that the Mexican train was to pass through Skeleton Canyon sooner than expected, Curly Bill was away on other business. His lieutenant, Jim Hughes, took charge and recruited seven of Galeyville's most unsavory characters for the job. Among these were two close friends, Billy Grounds and Zwing Hunt.

Knowing where the Mexicans usually paused for lunch and to give their mules a rest in the western end of the canyon, the outlaws concealed themselves behind rocks and settled down to wait. When the unsuspecting Mexicans appeared, the bandits counted 30 heavily laden mules—one of the richest trains even to pass along the Smuggler's Trail. As the Mexicans settled down to their siesta, a roar of gunfire broke from the canyon walls. Taken completely by surprise, the Mexicans scattered in panic. Mules not yet relieved of their packs stampeded in fright, spilling their contents across the canyon floor. Out of their ambush rode the yelling outlaws in pursuit.

After the outlaws gathered up the far-scattered loot, they found the quantity to be too large for their horses to carry to Galeyville. At the mouth of the canyon they dug a large pit and buried it until it could be recovered. No sooner were the outlaws back in their old haunt than Jim Hughes presented a plan to Hunt and Grounds to doublecross the gang and take all the treasure for themselves. While Hughes remained in Galeyville to allay any suspicions, they were to ride out to Skeleton Canyon and transfer the buried treasure to another hiding place. Only the three of them would then know where it was cached.

Accordingly, Hunt and Grounds employed an old Mexican with a team and wagon. They dug up the treasure at the eastern end of the canyon, hauled it farther into the canyon, and dumped it into another hole dug by the Mexican. The old man and his horses were then killed and dragged into the hole, which was filled in and covered over. The wagon was rolled over the spot and burned. Now only Hunt and Grounds knew where the treasure was buried.

Instead of returning immediately to Galeyville, Hunt and Grounds rode to the ranch of Jack Chandler near Charleston. Here they were surprised by a posse looking for them on a charge of rustling cattle. Billy Grounds was killed and Hunt was so badly wounded that he had to be taken to a hospital in Tombstone, where he was placed under guard. He was now the sole possessor of the secret treasure site.

When Jim Hughes heard of Hunt's predicament, he rushed to Tombstone to learn where the treasure was buried before Hunt might die. But Hunt had already eluded the guard and fled the scene. It was only now that Hughs realized that he, too, had been doublecrossed. The fate of Zwing Hunt has never been conclusively proven. His brother turned up in Tombstone sometime later and said that Hunt had been killed by Indians shortly after his escape from the hospital. Jim Hughes was one of those who doubted the story.

The story circulated that Hunt had not been killed at all, but had made his way to his home in San Antonio, Texas, where he shortly died of his wounds. It was said that before death came to the outlaw, he called in an uncle and gave him a map to the treasure site. The waybill placed the treasure at the foot of Davis Mountain, from the summit of which could be seen an open stretch of New Mexico to the east. A short distance from the mountain was a curving canyon, its west wall covered with trees and its east wall bare and rocky. Through the canyon meandered a small stream. A 10 ft. drop created a cascade, and near it were two small springs, one of which was called Silver and the other Gum. Twenty steps east of the actual treasure site was a square-shaped rock about three feet high. Over the burial spot would be found the irons of a burned wagon.

All one had to do, then, to find the Skeleton Canyon smuggler's treasure, which has been estimated as high as $3,000,000 in value, was to locate Davis Mountain. But Davis Mountain, it turned out, was one that Hunt and Grounds themselves had named in honor of a pal they had buried there. It could be any one of hundreds of peaks in the Peloncillas.

Hunt's uncle searched for the treasure without success, and it is said that Zwing's brother Hugh spent some 30 years trying to locate it. The two springs have never been located, nor has the waterfall. Possibly these have dried up. The remains of a burned wagon were found in Skeleton Canyon, but there was no treasure beneath it. A lone grave was found at the base of Harris Mountain, which some believed might be the so-called Davis Mountain, but the surrounding area did not fit the waybill, nor could the exhumed body be identified as that of Davis.

There is little question but that Galeyville outlaws ambushed and robbed a smuggling train in Skeleton Canyon. The bleached bones of dead smugglers and their mules were visible for many years, and an occasional Mexican coin is still found in the eastern entrance to Skeleton Canyon. About 1891, some 10 years after the ambush, a cowboy and a government official riding through Skeleton Canyon came upon an old rawhide pouch. The cowboy gave it a reckless kick and out poured several thousand dollars in Mexican coins.

ARIZONA

The 39 bars of gold, a cigar box filled with diamonds, two figures of pure gold, $90,000 in minted Mexican silver dollars and untold numbers of bags of gold coins may still rest in Skeleton Canyon. Many treasure stories are less well authenticated.

Cochise County—On the night of January 30, 1895, the westbound Southern Pacific passenger and express train was held up by four masked men along the northern edge of what is now known as Willcox Dry Lake, about five miles west of the town of Willcox. The Wells Fargo safe carried a shipment of gold coins and jewelry valued then at $84,000. On the floor of the express car were seven bags of silver pesos consigned to the Mexican government. Only the train's crew knew of its existence. Gaining access to the locked express car, the bandits set a charge of dynamite against the safe and tamped it with the bags of coins. When the explosion went off it devastated the express car, scattered silver pesos to the wind, and exposed the contents of the safe the bandits were after. They gathered up the loot and vanished into the darkness.

As soon as the train backed into Willcox and spread the alarm, Sheriff Fly rapidly organized a posse. Failing to pick up a trail, it returned to Willcox within hours. On the following day a rancher named Moore rode into Willcox and related that two men whom he recognized as Grant Wheeler and Joe George had stopped at his darkened house on the morning following the holdup and demanded a meal. As they rode away, he noted that their saddlebags were heavily loaded. On the same day another rancher named Yates reported that the same two men had stopped at his place, took fresh horses at rifle point, and rode away in the direction of Ruckers Canyon in the Dos Cabezas Mountains, a well known hideout of outlaws. Investigation revealed that Wheeler and George had stopped in Willcox on the morning of the holdup, and had purchased explosives, caps, fuses and ammunition at Soto's General Store, dropping the remark that they were going prospecting in the Dos Cabezas Mountains. The names of Wheeler and George were now definitely connected with the train robbery.

All efforts to locate the wanted men failed. Then, three months later, Wheeler turned up at his brother's ranch in the Blue Mountains of Utah. Upon being told that Utah lawmen were looking for him, Wheeler went to the corral to get his horse and move out. But the posse was there waiting for him. Wheeler drew his gun, placed it to his head and pulled the trigger. He had less than $1.00 in his pockets and his saddlebags were empty. Joe George was never seen again.

One theory has it that Wheeler and George had two accomplices in the holdup. They took the $84,000, rode into Willcox, hid it, and then joined the posse looking for Wheeler and George. Another theory is that Wheeler and George doublecrossed their accomplices, rode into the Dos Cabezas Mountains, hid the loot, after which Wheeler had killed George and gone to Utah to wait for things to blow over.

If the treasure is buried in the Dos Cabezas Mountains, as some still think, the most likely place is said to be a cave near two small peaks in the northern reaches of the mountains. Some years after the robbery, two prospectors stumbled upon a cave in this area, and while exploring it found two dust-covered saddles and bridles. Who could have lugged them up the mountain and abandoned them? Was it Grant Wheeler and Joe George, and if so, why?

Cochise County—On September 9, 1899, three masked men held up the westbound Southern Pacific Express as it stopped for water at the little town of Cochise eleven miles southwest of Willcox and but four miles from the site of the 1895 holdup reported above. Blasting open the express car, the bandits fled with a Wells Fargo shipment of $60,000 in gold bullion and coin. As soon as the news reached Willcox, Constable Burt Alvord formed a posse and rode to the scene of the crime. Splitting into three groups, Alvord led one while his two deputies, William N. "Billy" Stiles and Bob Downing, headed the others. When none of them picked up a trail they met at an appointed rendezvous and returned to Willcox.

But a resourceful Wells Fargo agent, John Thacker, refused to admit defeat. When word reached him days later that one of Alvor's deputies, Bob Downing, was spending new $10 gold pieces freely in the Willcox saloons, Thacker began a quiet investigation. He soon learned that all three of the Willcox peace officers had at one time or another been engaged in some form of outlawry.

Thacker went to work on Billy Stiles, whom he considered to be the weakest of the three. It was not long before he had a confession. Stiles revealed that he, Alvord and Downing had engineered the holdup, but that Alvord had taken no active part in it, the third man having been a cowboy named Burt Matts. After the holdup they had met Alvord at an abandoned shack along the old trail from Cochise to Willcox. Here each man had been given $350 from the stolen loot, with intsructions not to spend it in any manner that would attract attention. While the robbers slipped into a change of clothing Alvord had brought them, he rode off with the remainder of the loot and buried it.

It was now apparent to Thacker that only Alvord knew where the loot was hidden. On being promised leniency, Stiles agreed to assist the agent. Alvord, Matts and Downing were picked up and jailed. According to the agreed upon plan, Stiles was placed in a cell with Alvord, but instead of finding out where the treasure was hidden and passing the information along to Thacker, Stiles revealed his scheme. With the aid of a gun smuggled into the jail, Alvord and Stiles made their escape, taking with them a notorious Mexican outlaw named Augustine Chacon, a man badly wanted by the Arizona Rangers.

A few miles out of Willcox, Alvord and Stiles abandoned Chacon and the two fled to safety in Mexico, not pausing to recover the money. It was not long before Alvord was so badly wounded in a fight that he required medical attention. When Arizona authorities learned of this they managed to get word to Alvord that they would go easy on him if he would lure Chacon into Arizona where he could be arrested. Alvord agreed and went through with the plan. Chacon was captured and Alvord received a 10-year sentence.

In at attempt to get Alvord to reveal where the $58,950 was hidden, his sentence was delayed from time to time. But Alvord stubbornly refused to cooperate and was eventually sent to the Territorial Prison in Yuma. Meantime, the search for the treasure was pressed. Even Stiles, released from jail in return for the help he had given Thacker, joined the search. Nothing was found.

Alvord served his sentence and was released. Months later he appeared in Mexico, always under the surveillance of Wells Fargo agents. Suddenly he disappeared and was never seen in Arizona again. Years later officials learned that he had died in Panama. Reports indicated that if he wasn't a wealthy man, he certainly wasn't suffering from lack of funds. Had he managed to elude the Wells Fargo agents and recover the treasure? Some believe that he might have, but others think that the loot from the Cochise holdup is still buried along the old trail to Willcox.

Cochise County—About all that remains of the old ghost town of Charleston, which was too tough in its heyday for even Wyatt Earp, is a farmhouse, an abandoned railroad station, the ruins of an old mill and smelter, and crumbled adobe walls overgrown with mesquite. The ruins of the old mill's thick walls stand on the east side of the San Pedro River across from what was once the main part of the town—the saloons and honkytonks. This was the headquarters of the Tombstone Mining and Milling Co., its ore being freighted here from Tombstone where there was insufficient water. The "Big House" served as the company's office and assay quarters. One room contained a large steel vault where bullion was stored. Its door is now removed and a large hole has been hacked through the metal—the work of treasure seekers.

On a night during the height of the Tombstone mining boom, Billy Grounds, Zwing Hunt and one or two others held up the office of the mining company, killed the mine superintendent, and made away with a large amount of bullion carried on pack-horses. This bullion was never recovered, and many believe that it was buried nearby so it would be easily available to the robbers who made Charleston their headquarters. It is said that the bullion was never recovered because it was not too long after the robbery that all of the participants were killed or fled from the country.

Cochise County—The Can Can Restaurant building still stands at Fourth and Allen Streets in Tombstone. Abandoned now, it was once famed for its delicacies. In the 1880's its owner employed hunters to keep it supplied with deer, bear and antelope, and imported fish and lobsters from Guaymas, Mexico, by fast stage. It was during this era that a trusted employee stole a large amount of money. When apprehended, he readily admitted the crime, but refused to tell where the money was hidden.

Just before his death in prison, he revealed that he had buried the money in Boot Hill Graveyard at the northwestrn limits of the town. When a search was made and nothing was found, the embezzler elaborated by saying that he had chosen a burial site next to the grave of "Dutch Annie," a much admired and generous lady of the night. When a search here also proved fruitless, it was decided that the thief was deliberately withholding the hiding place, expecting to serve his sentence and then recover the money. He was in jail only a few weeks, however, when he suddenly took ill and died. It is believed that the Can Can Restaurant treasure has never been found.

Cochise County—What little remains of the once important town of Dos Cabezas is on State 186 about 16 miles southeast of Willcox. It is said that a Mexican wagon train loaded with a vast amount of gold bound for Santa Fe camped here at the springs one night. Because of the fear of robbery, the treasure was customarily unloaded each night and buried near the camp. Early on the following morning the camp was attacked by Indians, and only a 7-year-old boy managed to escape. Hiding in the bushes throughout the day, he was found by an aged Mexican and finally made his way back to Mexico. It is said that he made a search for the treasure some 45 years later, looking for it between two hills where the dry bed of the Willcox could be seen to the west. Believed never found, the treasure is said to have included a life-sized gold statue of the Virgin Mary, a huge gold crucifix and a great quantity of gold dust and nuggets.

Cochise County—Fort Huachuca was established as a camp in 1877 to protect settlers and travelers from the Apaches. In 1882 the camp was made permanent, but saw little military activity after Geronimo's surrender in 1886 until the Madera revolt in Mexico in 1911. It then became a base for border patrols. The fort, garrisoned by Negro troops during World War II, is now a U. S. Electronics Proving Ground. All this is a preface to saying that a treasure is supposed to be buried here—an enormous treasure that has been estimated in value at from $90,000,000 to $280,000,000. We don't know how those figures are arrived at.

In 1941 Private Robert Jones was stationed at Fort Huachuca. One Sunday he and a buddy, Sam Mays, decided to take a walk into the mountains. As Jones strolled ahead of Mays in Huachuca Canyon, the ground suddenly gave way under him and he fell into a deep pit. Probing about in the darkness, Jones' hands ran across some objects that felt to him like stacked bricks. He picked up one and was surprised at its weight. At this point Mays lowered a long piece of thick vine into the hole and Jones clambered up.

Hurrying back to the barracks, the two soldiers secured a flashlight and a long length of rope. A few hours later they were back at the pit and Jones was lowered into its depth. He found two rooms, obviously carved by hand out of natural caverns. In one of the rooms he found the heavy objects stacked in long rows. Some were grayish in color and others were a dull yellow. Jones suspected that the yellow bars were gold. With a hatchet, Jones chopped off a swo-pound chunk. Some days later Jones is said to have taken the chunk to an assayer in Douglas, but when this assayer was later identified and questioned he denied that he had ever seen Jones. Yet Jones persisted in saying the assayer had paid him $800 for the gold, half of which he had sent to his mother in Texas, and the other half he had spent on a party for his buddies.

Before Jones could return to the cavern again, he and Mays were transferred to different units and only saw each other occasionally. There was an agreement between them never to mention the find to anyone. Finally, Jones went to the still-open hole, pried a large boulder over it and carefully covered it with earth and stones. To mark the place he carved his initials in reverse—"JR" on a nearby rock.

When Jones' unit was shipped out to the South Pacific, he was left behind as unfit for combat duty. Mays—the only eyewitness to the discovery —was sent to the European Theater where he was killed in action. After the end of the war, Jones went to his home in Texas, but he could not forget his experience in Huachuca Canyon. Accompanied by two companions, he went to Fort Huachuca in 1959 and told his story to Col. Elbridge Bacon, Jr., who listened attentively enough but scoffed at the story. Nevertheless, he gave Jones and his friends permission to dig.

Noting that their progress was painfully slow, Col. Bacon, for some reason or another, ordered a bulldozer to the spot. At a depth of 12 feet water was struck and the work was called to a halt. Later a well-digging rig was brought in and at the 16-ft. level it broke into empty space. A clamshell scoop was now employed. It struck water at 32 feet, but continued until bedrock was reached. As a last resort dynamite was used, but when this failed to reveal the treasure, Col. Bacon permanently called off the Army's part in the search.

In 1963, with Jones seriously ill in Texas, the Army granted permission to explore to the Mahan Brothers Construction Co. After spending several thousand dollars on the venture, Mahan Brothers threw in the towel. In 1969 Robert Jones died, and the saga of the Fort Huachuca treasure was apparently ended.

During the excitement over the supposed millions in gold and silver bars in Huachuca Canyon, hardly anyone speculated as to where it had come from. Then, on Feb. 21, 1963, the Sierra Vista (Texas) *Gateway Times* (now defunct) attributed the treasure to the notorious Estrada Gang of Texas outlaws. No reason was given for this conclusion so it must be assumed that this was possibly a wild guess. In 1874, the Estrada gang, joined by a band of American outlaws from the Tombstone, Arizona, area, did conduct a successful raid on the mint at Monterrey, Mexico, and did make their way into Texas with an enormous amount of loot. But this treasure was traditionally believed buried in the region of El Muerto Springs, in Jeff Davis County, Texas, as related in "A Guide to Treasure in Texas" (True Treasure Library). The mystery of the supposed Fort Huachuca treasure is still unsolved.

Coconino or Apache County—In 1863-64, Kit Carson and a party of soldiers marched the entire length of Arizona's Canyon de Chelly, rounding up 7,000 Navajo Indians for the "Long Walk" to the Bosque Redondo in New Mexico. Two of the men in this military party were named Mitchell and Merrick. Their first names are hardly ever agreed upon. They noted the abundance of silver jewelry and ornaments worn by some of the Indian captives and guessed that it came from the Navajo lands to the northwest. Many of the Indians who had sought refuge in Canyon de Chelly were from the Monument Valley region of Arizona and Utah. Mitchell and Merrick asked questions and came to the conclusion that all of the Indians from Monument Valley were richly draped in silver, therefore, they must have a source of silver in the land of monuments, an isolated country where rose-colored pinnacles loomed above the desert floor like Greek temples.

At the end of the Long Walk, the enlistment terms of Mitchell and Merrick were up and they were mustered out of service. Posing as trappers, they entered Monument Valley and went through the motions of operating trap lines, while they were actually searching for the source of the Navajo silver. Observed in the area, they were warned to leave by aging Chief Hoskinini. The white men agreed to leave, but once out of the sight of the Indians, they continued their search.

At length Mitchell and Merrick found the silver mine of the Navajos. After taking out samples of the rich ore which they concealed in their packs, they started to leave but had not gone far when they were again stopped by the Indians. Told that they had been seen taking out the ore, they were given permission to keep it, but warned that if they were caught in the region again they would be killed.

The two prospectors went directly to Cortez, Colorado, where they told of their rich find and showed samples to prove it. They were financially unable to develop the mine they said, and were ready to team up with a few partners. They found no backers. They went to Mancos and told their story there, again with negative results. They repeated it in Dolores. Nobody wanted anything to do with their mine in the Navajo country.

It was not until 1879 that an interested party approached them. He was Jim Jarvis, a new arrival in Cortez. He had the original samples assayed and they ran $800 to the ton. Jarvis proposed to back the prospectors with $6,000 provided they would return to the mine and bring out additional ore to substantiate their story. If they brought back the same kind of ore, he would put up money for a fifty percent interest in the venture.

Mitchell and Merrick accepted the offer. Although several years had passed since they had last been in Monument Valley, they had no trouble in locating the silver ore. They saw no Indians and wondered if they had left Monument Valley. After mining all the ore they could pack, they set out again for Colorado. One night they made camp at the base of a great red butte. No longer afraid of the Indians, their campfire glowed brightly. But in the shadows the red-men waited in silence for the signal to attack. Unseen by the prospectors, the Indians had watched their every move.

One of the prospectors had not yet fallen asleep when he thought he heard a faint unfamiliar sound in the night. He reached out an arm to arouse his partner. At that moment the lurking Indians swarmed upon them. Both men jumped to their feet. Merrick was immediately killed, but Mitchell, although painfully wounded, managed to reach the shadows and disappear into the darkness. Somehow he managed to crawl through the night, crossing four miles of sand to the talus base of another great butte. Sunrise found him huddled among some rocks, and it was there that the Indians put him out of his misery. Each prospector had met death at the base of a red butte. Today one is known as Merrick Butte, the other as Mitchell Butte—monuments to a lost mine.

When Mitchell and Merrick did not return to Cortez, their intended backer made inquiries. He heard rumors that they had been killed, that they had been wounded but were alive, that they were lost, and that they were running out on him. Finally Jarvis formed a party of 22 men and they rode into Monument Valley to investigate. They talked to the Navajos who said little, but led them to two separate graves four miles apart. The bodies were exhumed and identified as those of Mitchell and Merrick. At the base of Merrick Butte they found the rich ore samples and some of the prospectors' belongings.

Charged with the murder of the two white men, the Navajos vehemently denied it, placing the blame on a party of Paiutes. Chief Hoskinini made such a good case for his own people that the charges were dropped. After re-burying the two bodies, the Jarvis party, unhindered by the Navajos, made a futile search for the silver before it returned to Colorado. The Indians are believed to have then obliterated all traces of the mine lest it attract an influx of white men into the region.

This, then, is the popular version of the Mitchell-Merrick Lost Mine. There are many variations of the story but they are essentially the same. The murder of Mitchell and Merrick is a matter of historical record, but whether or not they found silver ore in Monument Valley is a point still argued. However, some people in a position to know some of the firsthand facts, believe they did. One of these was Henry Goulding, operator of Goulding's Trading Post in Monument Valley. He probably knew the Navajos better than any white man in the area, and the Indians trusted him.

TREASURE GUIDE

Goulding would never reveal what the Indians told him, but it is known that he, too, searched for silver in Monument Valley.

Hoskinini-begay, son of old Chief Hoskinini, told Charles Kelly, who later became Superintendent of Capitol Reef National Monument in Utah, that he remembered the two prospectors and the incident of their death at the hands of the Paiutes. He stated that the white men had with them "sacks of rocks." When Kelly asked Hoskinini-begay if it was true that the Navajos had a secret silver mine, he replied, "It is true." He went on to explain that originally only seven tribal members knew its exact location. One by one they grew old and died, but just before the death of the last survivor, he passed along the secret to his son. The son was never able to locate the mine, and in this manner, it became lost even to the Navajos—until it was discovered by Mitchell and Merrick.

Coconino County—In 1879 four bandits held up a stage near Gila Bend and secured $125,000 worth of gold coins and 22 gold ingots each stamped with the word "AJO," the mining district from which they originated. The following day the same outlaws robbed another stage near Stanwix Station in western Maricopa County, securing two more iron chests containing $140,000 in gold coin and $60,000 in currency. Fleeing northeastward, the bandits were trailed into the Tonto Basin country, where tracks also revealed that they were being followed by a band of Apaches. Followed northwestward from this point, the posse overtook the outlaws and in the shootout that resulted, they assumed that all the outlaws were killed.

But unknown to the posse, two of the original holdup men did escape and made their way to the small camp that later became the town of Holbrook, Navajo County, and holed up to wait for things to blow over. Here one of the bandits was killed in a poker game, leaving only one who knew where the treasure was cached. This man was Henry Tice, and angered over his partner's death, he deliberately murdered the gambler. Tice was arrested and jailed. Securing a gun in some manner, he forced his way out of the jail and walked straight into the hands of a waiting mob that killed him. In this manner died the only man who knew where the treasure was hidden.

The many searches that have been made for this treasure, estimated at being worth well over $400,000, has centered around the cliffs between Mormon Lake and Flagstaff.

Coconino County—In 1902, freight wagons loaded with 3,300 pounds of mercury left the Colorado River area north of Lee's Ferry headed for Flagstaff, where the mercury would be transshipped by rail. The mercury was packed in iron tubes each six inches in diameter and 10 feet long. Twenty-six of the tubes were loaded aboard the wagons, but when they were unloaded in Flagstaff, six of the tubes were found to be missing. Freighters denied any knowledge of the shortage, but it was obvious that somebody was withholding the truth. In time rumors spread that the missing pipes of mercury had been unloaded at Bitter Springs about 15 miles south of Lee's Ferry. The mercury in them was estimated to have a value of $65,000.

Some years later it was reported by some Indians who had observed the hiding of the tubes from a distance that they were buried in sand at the base of Echo Cliffs. Adding to the mystery, the Indians said there were ten of the tubes. Following this clue, Abe Cole made an extensive search for miles along the base of Echo Cliffs and finally located the ends of some of the tubes emerging from the sand. Because of their weight and the depth to which they were covered, Cole was unable to remove them. He was driven from the site by one of the frequent sandstorms that sweep the area. When he returned, prepared to dig out the mercury-filled tubes, he was unable to locate them. The storm had completely recovered them, and there they probably will remain until another storm exposes them to view.

Coconino County—Capt. W. H. Hardy established a trading post and ferry on the Colorado River at the head of steamboat navigation in 1864. It was an extensive place with a mill for crushing the ore Hardy hoped prospectors would bring in from the surrounding country. Gold and silver were known to exist in the hills around Hardyville, as the place came to be known, and an occasional prospector drifted in with some ore, but the fear of the Indians kept most prospectors out of the area. Hardy's mill was mostly idle. In 1873 it was destroyed by fire and never rebuilt.

One day in 1866 an old prospector ambled into Hardy's store, outfitted himself for a trip into the mountains, loaded down his burros and departed. A few weeks later he returned with rich specimens of gold and silver. He told Capt. Hardy that he had found the ore at the mouth of the Little Colorado River, and he described his find in glowing terms as a "mountain of silver."

Hardy, an experienced mining man, estimated the ore to assay at $7,000 to the ton, and he purchased the ore at that price. The prospector took his money and immediately bought passage on the next steamer down the Colorado. Hide nor hair of him was never seen around Hardyville again; nor did Hardy much care, for he was certain that he could find the "mountain of silver."

Hardy organized a party of prospectors and they scoured a large area at the junction of the two Colorados. Eventually they gave up and returned to the post empty-handed. Hardy now conceded that the old prospector might have lied to him. If so, where did he get the ore? And why did he fail to return and work his find? Those who guessed that the prospector had probably stolen the ore were probably right. Veracity is not a virtue attributed to old prospectors.

Coconino County—When the Star Stage Line coach pulled into Pine

Springs Station, there was no one to greet it except a party of masked men who knew exactly what they were looking for—three iron chests each containing $75,000 in gold coins. The shipment had been kept a highly guarded secret, but apparently there had been a leak somewhere along the line.

As the horses reared to a stop, the lone passenger was dropped from his seat alongside the driver, a veteran named Stacey. Somehow Stacey managed to escape the hail of bullets, rolled from the stage and scampered for cover in the nearby grove of pines. Grabbing one of the bolting horses, he mounted and galloped off to spread the alarm. He had not gone far when he met a posse in search of some other outlaws a few miles away. Changing their plans, the posse headed full speed for the stage station.

Having dragged the three chests into the station, the outlaws were apparently trying to open them when the members of the posse rode up. They were immdiately fired upon from the station and took cover. The siege, starting in late morning, lasted into the night, and the robbers were not dislodged until the station was set afire. One by one, as the robbers fled in the light of the burning building, they were mowed down, five in number.

Certain that the chests would be found in the burned-out building, the men entered and made a search as soon as the embers had cooled down. Not a sign of the treasure chests could be found! Nor did extensive digging and searching uncover them.

Ensuing months of searching, in which the building was virtually demolished and every foot of soil beneath its floor exposed to bedrock, revealed nothing. The area surrounding the station was probed and dug until hardly a foot of soil remained unturned. Nothing was ever found. Many theories were presented, examined and investigated, yet the $225,000 hoard remained wherever the outlaws had placed it. It was the final opinion of many that the chests had been hurriedly dropped into a nearby natural crevice before the posse had arrived, and that an earthquake had later closed the crevice.

The site of Pine Springs (not to be confused with the Pine Springs near Williams) may still be located, and perhaps the best way to do that is to inquire in the little town of Happy Jack.

Coconino County—In 1879 Capt. Charles Watt and Irwin Baker shared a cabin in a gulch near where Cripple Creek, Colorado, now stands. Baker had samples of gold ore which he claimed to have picked up with a Mexican in Arizona. The site was located on an Indian reservation and the Indians had chased them out. The Mexican later died of wounds he had received in the fight, and this left Baker sole possessor of the mine's location.

The ore was white quartz richly threaded with beads and strings of gold. Baker stated that there was a vast quantity of it under a shelving rock which showed signs of once having been the home of cliff dwellers. He had carefully mapped the country and kept the chart among his possessions, which amounted to a battered valice and some mining tools.

ARIZONA

In the fall of 1879, Baker left the cabin to make a trip to Leadville afoot. There he contracted pneumonia and died. When no relatives appeared to claim his belongings, Capt. Watt appropriated the valise and searched it for the map Baker had told him he possessed. Finding nothing, he concluded Baker had taken it with him to Leadville. He forgot the matter.

About ten years later, Watt needed a strap of leather and decided to cut one from Baker's old valise which was still in his possession. The first slash of his knife revealed, between the outside leather and the lining, a yellowed piece of paper. It was the map Irwin Baker had concealed there. The chart had been prepared with care and many landmarks were well indicated. Capt. Watt figured he would have no trouble in locating the vein of white quartz under the shelving ledge. He immediately formed a search party which included Robert McReynolds (who later recorded an account of the search in his book, "Thirty Years on the Frontier"), John Bowden, a mining engineer, but unfamiliar with the southwestern country, and a Capt. Baker who was no relation to Irwin Baker.

Within a short time they were en route to the Coconino country in Arizona, making their way toward Lava Butte, which was the key landmark to the lost mine. One night they camped within sight of Lava Butte, everyone in a joyous mood because the following day would bring them to the rich ore. After the evening meal, John Bowden left for a short walk. He was cautioned not to stray too far away. He never came back.

The delay caused by Bowden's disappearance used up the party's remaining water and provisions and their situation became desperate. Robert McReynolds went out alone to search for Bowden and himself became lost. His horse dropped dead, but McReynolds was eventually found by other members of the party.

Bowden's body was later found a full five miles from the camp, and it was assumed that he had died of exposure, there being no marks on his body. Before the party could reorganize, Capt. Watt took ill and died. He was the sole possessor of the map and it could not be found on his body nor among his effects. The expedition was abandoned and so far as it is known, the Lost Valise Mine has never been found.

Coconino County—Mormon Mountain lies about 26 miles southeast of Flagstaff, and just to the north of Mormon Lake, one of Arizona's most popular summer playgrounds. When Mormons settled the area, silver was found on Mormon Mountain by Ike Roberts and Jim Taylor. Many people in Flagstaff and the little Mormon village saw samples of the ore, but the two miners kept the exact location of the mine a secret, carefully concealing their trail when they entered and left the mountains. Believing their ore to be of little value, Taylor and Roberts eventually abandoned it and disappeared. However, when samples left behind in Flagstaff were assayed they proved to be rich in silver, spurring an extensive search for the Mormon Mountain lost mine. It has never been found.

TREASURE GUIDE

Coconino County—According to legend, a Mexican shepherd girl was one day herding her goats in the area south of Williams and west of Turkey Spring. Caught in a sudden sandstorm, she took refuge in a slight depression, and with her back to the wind, prepared to sit out the storm. Pushing aside some loose rocks at her feet, she noted a glitter of yellow. She examined one and found it to be filled with gold. Picking up others, she realized she was sitting in a basin filled with gold nuggets!

Trying to locate her herd after the storm subsided, the girl became completely lost, unable to recognize a single landmark. While pondering her desperate situation, she heard the faint whistle of a train in the distance. Following the horizon with her eyes, she finally picked out the trail of smoke from a locomotive. Across the desert she picked her way until she finally came to the railroad tracks. Knowing that the train had long since passed, she settled down to wait for another. Hours passed, but another train eventually arrived and stopped in response to her distress signal.

Safely aboard the train, she told her story to members of the crew and showed the nuggets that she had brought with her to prove it. Later, when she tried to lead a party of searchers to the gold-filled basin, she had to admit finally that she was just as lost as on that day when she had been caught in the storm.

It is believed that a cowboy stumbled upon the basin later, but he was out of water and his horse was about to drop of exhaustion. He, too, left the gold behind and was never able to locate the spot again.

Coconino County—When an enormous meteor crashed on the Coconino Pleteau near Winslow, Arizona, an estimated 22,000 years ago, it created a crater 4,000 feet across and 570 feet deep, and scattered fragments over an area 2½ miles in diameter. It is believed that the main body of the meteor perhaps a mile deep, may be worth as much as $20,000,000 because of the many diamonds it might contain.

Dolph Cannon, a mysterious character who lived the life of a recluse in the caves of Canyon Diablo, spent many years gathering meteor fragments, breaking them apart and extracting the tiny diamonds. When he appeared in Winslow on frequent trading trips, he always carried a large roll of bills. Some thought this money was secured from selling the diamonds he recovered, but some believed he had entered the country with a supply of money which he kept cached in one of the caves.

While Cannon was observed several times crushing the meteor fragments to secure the diamonds, others who tried it had no success. One day Cannon disappeared and was never again seen in his canyon haunts. It was speculated that he had accumulated a fortune in diamonds and had left the country as mysteriously as he had originally appeared. Some 10 years later, it was learned that he had been murdered, supposedly by someone attempting to force him to tell where his accumulation of meteor diamonds was cached. Many subsequent searches of Canyon Diablo revealed the caves in which the recluse had lived, but no diamonds or cash is believed to have ever been found.

Coconino County—About 1872, a Missourian named John Hix teamed up with an old prospector named Lemuel Dodson, more commonly known as "Jackass" Dodson. The two left Tucson together, following Dodson's directions for he had some definite ideas of the area in which he wanted to prospect, while Hix seems not to have cared as long as they found gold. Dodson's plan took them to an Indian village about 40 miles north of Flagstaff.

Here Dodson met an Indian girl. From their actions, Hix assumed they had met before, but Dodson was uncommunicative on the subject. After some lengthy talks with the friendly Indian girl, Dodson informed his partner that she had agreed to guide them to a place where there was plenty of gold nuggets in the bed of a dry stream.

When all was ready they left the village and worked their way to the northwest where they made camp at a waterhole. From here the girl pointed to the distant mountains and said that was where the gold would be found. She also warned that it was a waterless area and they would have to take a generous supply.

On the following day they reached the mountains and made camp. The girl refused to go farther, but gave the men detailed instructions as to where they would locate the dry stream bed. They found it without any trouble and noted that the nuggets apparently came from a vein along the bank of the wash. In following up the vein, hoping to find its source, they heard the girl's faint screams from the camp. Rushing to her aid, they found her safe and sound. She could not explain her fright.

On the following night they were awakened by strange sounds. An investigation revealed nothing and they settled down again, concluding that the sounds had come from prowling night animals. In the morning they made the horrible discovery that their water bags had been emptied, leaving them with only a half gallon. Then it was learned that their burros were missing. Hix remained in the camp with the girl while Dodson went out in search of them.

The last of the water was gone on the third day, and Dodson had not returned. They waited two more days and still he did not show up. Their situation was now desperate. They set out wearily to trail Dodson. Before the day's travel was over, the girl collapsed and Hix had to make camp. Leaving her alone, he went in search of water, but became hopelessly lost. He was at the point of exhaustion when he stumbled upon the waterhole where they had originally filled their water bags. But with absolutely nothing in which to carry water, he could not return for the girl—even if he could find his way. Instead, he started for the Indian village for help.

After a brief rest, Hix and five Indians left in search of the girl and Dodson. They came across the old prospector's body. Two bullet holes plainly indicated the manner in which he had died, but there were no clues as to the identity of the killer. The search for the girl continued, but her disappearance was complete. Nor could Hix locate the dry wash with the nuggets and its nearby vein.

The murder of Dodson and the disappearance of the Indian girl were never solved, but some suspicion was cast upon a young Indian, who it is thought may have been in love with the girl and jealous of Dodson. It was conjectured that he had followed the party into the mountains, emptied their waterbags at night, drove away the burros and killed Dodson when he went in search of them. Supposedly he had returned later and killed the girl. He was never confronted with the crime, and the bed of gold nuggets has never been found.

Coconino County—On the morning of May 10, 1881, five masked men held up the Canyon Diablo-Flagstaff stage about 30 miles east of Flagstaff. The driver, "Cap" John Hance, tried to convince the outlaws that there was no treasure aboard the stage, but the outlaws seemed to know exactly what they were after—the two mail sacks. These sacks contained two 5-gallon oak kegs packed with a Wells Fargo shipment of small gold ingots and gold coins consigned to a San Francisco bank. The sacks had been filled in with old newspapers to make them look like regular sacks of mail, a scheme devised by Wells Fargo agents. Many outlaws would not touch U. S. Mail sacks. The reported value of the gold was $125,000.

A hurriedly organized posse rode out in search of the robbers, but soon returned to report that the trail had been lost. Sometime later two Indian scouts working for the Army picked up the outlaws' trail and followed it into the mountains near Flagstaff. Returning to their base, they reported that the bandits were holed up in a log cabin located in heavy timber at a place later to become known as Viet Spring. In the nearby corral stood five horses. A detachment of soldiers headed out for the outlaw rendezvous, arriving just as the men were mounting up in the corral. Ordered to throw down their guns, the bandits opened fire. It was returned by the troopers and in a few minutes the five stage robbers were dead. Not a trace of the loot was found.

Repeated searches were made for the treasure, and when George Viet acquired the property several years later, he devoted many years to a futile search, exploring every ice cavern in the area he could find. He did locate signs on rocks in the region, but it is not known that they had any connection with the treasure.

Over the years various strange characters turned up in Flagstaff, made fruitless searches and then disappeared. Then a local man, Jim McGuire, who was seldom known to have the price of a beer, started spending $50 gold coins in the saloons. When asked to tell where he got them, he would only say, "I found them!" When McGuire dropped dead in one of the saloons one day, and no wealth was found among his meager belongings, it was guessed that he had indeed found the stagecoach loot, but had only taken a few coins at a time, concealing the remainder. In recent years many searches have been made with metal detectors, but the treasure has apparently eluded everyone.

Coconino County—Roy Gardner, mail and train robber, and "escape artist" extraordinary, started his career of crime in 1906 when he deserted the U. S. Army. After mining for a couple of years in New Mexico, he became a gunrunner out of Arizona for the Carranza forces in Mexico. It was during this period that Gardner is said to have concealed $16,000 in gold coins in the cone of an extinct volcano near Flagstaff. It is believed that the outlaw never got around to recovering this treasure, although he was in Arizona at later dates. In 1921 he was captured in an attempted train robbery in Phoenix and sentenced to 75 years in prison. He was paroled in 1938, and in 1940, broke and with impaired vision, he committed suicide.

Coconino County—In 1887, Samuel Clevenger, an Arizona rancher, sold his cattle in Spofford for $2,000 in gold. Loading their possessions on a wagon, Clevenger, his wife and an adult daughter, Jessie, started for Oregon where they planned to resume ranching. Two cowboys named Wilson and Johnson trailed along hearding 100 head of horses. Mrs. Clevenger placed the $2,000 in a baking soda can and hid it in the wagon by day, but buried it at night at a place near their camp.

After a few weeks of uneventful travel, the Clevengers reached Lee's Ferry, crossed the Colorado River and made camp along the old trail just south of the Utah border. On the following morning one of the cowboys brutally murdered Sam Clevenger with an axe, and the women fled in panic. Overtaking Mrs. Clevenger, she too, was murdered. The cowboys found Jessie hiding in the bushes. She was seized and tortured in an attempt to make her tell where the gold was hidden. She, of course, did not know. After a fruitless search the men burned the wagon with the Clevenger's possession, forced Jessie to mount a horse, and ride off to the north, driving the horses before them.

It was two months before the remains of the burned wagon and the two shallow graves were found. Eventually, the killers were traced to Idaho and arrested. Strangely, Jessie Clevenger was living with the murderers, apparently making no effort to escape. Wilson confessed to committing the killings and was hanged. Johnson served a few years in prison for his part in the crime and was released. It is said that Jessie and many others later searched for the baking soda can of gold coins, but it is believed that it was never found.

Coconino County—On the morning of June 21, 1928, two small-time crooks, Earl Nelson and Willard F. Forrester, held up the Bank of Arizona

TREASURE GUIDE

in Clarkdale, Yavapai County, and dashed out to their getaway car with a sack containing $50,000. The mad rush to the car attracted the attention of Deputy Sheriff Jim Roberts, an old-time western peace officer. Just as the car roared away, Roberts brought it to a crashing halt with a bullet through Forrester's head. Nelson was captured and the $50,000 recovered.

Sentenced to 40 years in prison, Nelson later made a spectacular escape. When recaptured many miles north of the prison in Florence, Nelson said he was trying to make his way to Stoneman Lake, Coconino County, to recover several thousand dollars he and his partner had hidden just before going to the Clarkdale job. The money was from a previous robbery, and they did not want to have it on them in case they were picked up and questioned.

Several searches were made for the Stoneman Lake treasure following Nelson's statement, but nothing is known to have been found. He was not taken to the scene to point out the hiding place, which indicates to some that law enforcement officers placed little credence in his story. Nelson was paroled from prison in 1942, and it is not known whether or not he ever recovered the Stoneman Lake treasure.

Coconino County—A wagon train was attacked by Indians in Chavez Pass, about 30 miles from Winslow, in 1878. The two survivors later reported that the combined wealth of the eight wagons had been buried near the camp the night before the attack, a common practice among pioneer travelers. Although the site of the burned wagons is said to have been found by treasure hunters many years later, no treasure was found.

Coconino County—The old Tip Top Mine was located near the town of Gillette, now a ghost, in the southern reaches of the Bradshaw Mountains. When an accumulation of gold bars was ready for shipment, the bars were stacked like bricks in front of the company's mill office to await the stage to pick them up and transport them to Prescott. On a cold day in 1881, the guard assigned to watch them strolled over the the blacksmith shop to warm himself, leaving the bars unguarded. During his absence two outlaws, Henry Corey and Ralph Gaines, happened to ride by. They couldn't believe what they saw. There were the gold bars completely unguarded!

Deciding to take a chance on stealing a few of the bars. Gaines sneaked eight of the 38 bars out of sight. Meantime Corey went to the company's barn and secured two mules with packsaddles and panniers. Completely unobserved, the outlaws loaded the eight bars of gold and rode away. It was not until the stage driver refused to sign a receipt for 38 bars of gold that the stolen bars were missed. But no one had the slightest idea what had happened to them!

When it was learned that Corey and Gaines had stopped in Gillette to make some purchases the day of the robbery, suspicion was cast in their direction. It was only a hunch on the part of authorities, but word was

28

passed along that the pair was wanted for questioning about the missing gold bars

Driven out of their hideout in the Bradshaw Mountains by heavy snows, Corey and Gaines holed up in an abandoned cabin on Rogers Lake. About broke and in need of provisions, they buried the gold bars near the cabin and rode to Flagstaff to see what they could promote. Here they learned that they were suspects in the gold robbery. They also learned that a shipment of gold and silver coins would leave Flagstaff that night by stage. Successfully holding up the stage, they secured $25,000. Filling their pockets with what they could carry, the remainder of the loot was cached until they could reclaim it later. After remaining holed up for a few days, the bandits recovered the stage cache, took it to Rogers Lake, placed it in wooden kegs together with the eight bars of gold, and lowered it into the lake through a hole chopped into the ice.

As the weeks went by the outlaws became bolder, and frequented Flagstaff more often. Eventually their reckless spending of gold coins attracted the attention of the sheriff, who learned that the men were living in a cabin on Rogers Lake. Riding out to the cabin, he found no one there, but observed that the brands on the two mules in the cabin corral were strange to the area. He later traced the brands to the Tip Top Mining Company, thus definitely connecting Corey and Gaines to the theft of the gold bars. When the posse rode out to capture the outlaws, Corey and Gaines observed their approach in time to mount their horses and flee. But they had no time to recover the submerged coins and bars.

Taking refuge in the then new town of Holbrook, it was not long before Gaines was killed in a gambling brawl. Corey drifted around Arizona, committing minor crimes, and was never quite able to get back to recover the Rogers Lake loot. He was finally arrested for his part in a silver bullion robbery near Globe. He was sentenced to 20 years in the Territorial Prison at Yuma. Here he is said to have met an old friend who, before being released, was given directions to the Rogers Lake loot, together with instructions to recover it and use it in an effort to get Corey's prison sentence reduced. The sunken treasure was never located.

Upon Corey's release from prison 24 years later, he and the friend made repeated searches for the loot whenever they could do so without being observed. Corey died in 1936, and the friend who knew the secret died a few years later. Many searches have been made since their deaths, but the treasure is believed never to have been found.

Coconino County—The story of the John D. Lee Lost Mine begins with the Mountain Meadows Massacre in 1857, a black page in western history in which John Doyle Lee was a leading figure. During the period of Mormon migration to Utah, a party of 140 men, women and children, known as Frencher's Company, came to Salt Lake City. The section of Arkansas from which they had come had been the scene of the slaying of a Mormon apostle. Finding itself unwelcome in Salt Lake City, the Frencher party pushed southward, headed for California. In September they halted to rest at the little settlement of Mountain Meadows, about 30 miles south of Cedar City.

Isaac C. Haight, Mormon leader in the area, decided that the members of the Frencher company were heretics, and gave orders to John D. Lee, one of his subordinates, to kill them.

Lee assigned the task to a band of Paiute Indians who attacked the camp and killed seven men before they returned the fire and drove them off. After this defeat, Lee recruited about 100 Indians and 75 Mormons and renewed the attack. While Lee and the Mormons waited to the rear, the Indians maneuvered and poured a deadly fire into the camp. Again the massed fire of the Frenchers drove them off. Haight railed at the bungling and ordered Lee to get on with the matter of disposing of the "heretics."

A few days later, Lee and a companion visited the emigrant camp under a flag of truce. They assured the Frenchers that if they would abandon their wagons and arms, they would be guaranteed safe conduct through the Mormon settlements. After a parley, the Frenchers agreed to disarm themselves. Almost immediately they marched into an ambush of Paiutes and Mormons, many of the latter disguised as Indians. Of the 140 people, all excepting 17 children were slain in cold blood. It was 21 years before anyone paid for the murders.

In 1872 the United States Government finally got around to gathering evidence, and Lee's friends advised him to flee Utah Territory before he was arrested. He selected an isolated spot where Paria Creek empties into the Colorado River just above Marble Canyon in Arizona. To this ideally located hideout, which he called Lonely Dell, he brought two of his wives, Rachel and Emma, leaving 17 more behind in Utah. Here Lee built a house, a fort and eventually established a ferry across the Colorado over which he aided many of his companions in the massacre to escape into the wilds of northern Arizona.

Lee explored Grand Canyon methodically for mineral deposits. Although his movements at this time are understandably vague, it is believed that he was the first white man to visit the Havasupai Indians, being taken captive and living with them for two years. During his captivity it is thought that he discovered rich deposits of ore.

Robert B. Hildebrand, who went to live with Lee when he was a boy of 15, always insisted that Lee had a rich mine somewhere in Grand Canyon, but he did not know its exact location. Lee kept a journal in which he entered accounts of many of his activities, but these were either destroyed or lost. In a letter written to one of his daughters while he was imprisoned in Salt Lake City, he mentioned his "gold ledges."

In November, 1874, while visiting some of his scattered wives in Panguitch, Utah, Lee was arrested and later brought to trial in Beaver. In this trial the jury disagreed, and Lee, free on bail, returned to his ferry on the

Colorado. At the second trial he was found guilty and sentenced to death. In March, 1877, John D. Lee was executed for his part in the Mountain Meadows massacre, the only person to be punished for the crime.

Even before Lee's death the search was on for his lost mine, spurred by the finding of some rich ore on his property at Lee's Ferry. Facing death, Lee refused to deny or admit that he had a mine or mines in Arizona. It was about this time that a man named Brown claimed to have certain knowledge that Lee's mine was located in the Grand Canyon near the mouth of the Little Colorado River. The site is often said to be within view of Vulcan's Throne, which is on the north side of the Colorado, about six miles southeast of Mt. Emma.

Brown claimed also that Lee had buried seven cans of gold dust near the mine. It turned out that "Brown" was really Isaac C. Haight, Lee's former superior and the man who ordered the Mountain Meadows massacre. The information may have been given to him by Lee, but it is not believed that he ever found the mine or the seven tins of gold.

After the execution of John D. Lee, Emma Lee continued to live at Lee's Ferry, but eventually moved to Holbrook, Arizona, where she married Franklin French, pioneer stockman and miner. Relying on information supplied to him by Emma, French made many trips into Grand Canyon searching for Lee's mine. It is believed that he had no success.

Coconino County—Around 1868, a German named Herman Wolf, about whose early life very little is known, opened a trading post on the Little Colorado River northeast of the town of Canyon Diablo. He remained there until his death in 1899. During all this time he was never known to have banked any money. When he died it is believed that he left buried between $25,000 and $50,000 in or near the post which is now in ruins. Many searches have been made at the site and some old coins have been found, but it is thought that the main cache is still there.

Coconino County—A member of an outlaw gang named Louis Brown took refuge in the depths of Grand Canyon where he posed for several years as a miner, becoming known as Louie the Hermit. Brown is said to have taken $150,000 in gold and silver coins into the canyon with him, the proceeds of a train robbery in the Tucson area in which he had doublecrossed his partners. It is believed that Brown cached the loot in several different locations, on the theory that if any of his ex-partners caught up with him he could point out one cache and pretend that was all. They did catch up with him in 1889 and killed him, apparently getting only a small part of the loot.

Many searches for the Hermit's treasure were made, it is said, before Grand Canyon became a National Monument in 1908, and some secret searches after it was made a Nationl Park, and small amounts of coins are said to have been found from time to time.

31

TREASURE GUIDE

Coconino County—Various versions of this, tale have persisted in the Southwest for as long as white men can remember, handed down apparently, by the Indians from generation to generation. They all concern the rumors of a rich mine located near a red hill (**cerro colorado**) at the foot of a blue mountain (**sierra azul**). For many years this description was believed to fit a place in the Hopi country in northeastern Arizona.

After the Pueblo Indian uprising in 1680, in which the Spanish were either driven out of New Mexico or killed, the Spanish viceroy at Mexico City appointed, in 1690, Diego da Vargas (his full name was Don Diego de Vargas Zapata Lujan Ponce de Leon) as Governor of New Mexico. His job, of course, was to reconquer New Mexico and bring the Indians again under Spanish domination. Vargas established his headquarters at Paseo del Norte where he was installed in 1691. While here he received a letter from the Viceroy, the Count de Galva, instructing him to investigate rumors of rich silver or gold mines to the north.

Vargas did not have the slightest idea where the mines were located, so he called an assembly of all the people who might have some knowledge of the deposits and made them swear under oath to reveal everything they knew. No one, it seems, had any definite knowledge, but several, perhaps to save their skins or to ingratiate themselves to the new governor, professed to have distant friends who knew the locations of the mines. They decided that the area to be searched was a part of what is now the State of Arizona.

As a result of the meager information gathered, Vargas was authorized to make his famous **entrada** into New Mexico, later extending it into eastern Arizona. The only accomplishment was the exploration of a lot of new country. No mines were ever found, but Vargas concluded from the journey that the blue mountain (**sierra azul**) was the San Francisco peaks, which actually appear blue under certain conditions, and that the red hill (**cerro colorado**) was the red of the cinder cones northeast of Flagstaff. There is a great deal of country in between these points, but Vargas did not pause to search farther.

This whole region of Arizona is rich in legends of mines found and lost, and this is one of the oldest, dating back to 1662. Unlike most of the others, however, references to this lost mine or mines is said to be found in old Spanish documents.

Coconino County—There has long been a tradition of a cave of silver on the side of Elden Mountain northeast of Flagstaff. A prospector named Teller is said to have learned of the cave from Havasupai Indians, who are supposed to have obtained silver from the cave which they hammered into ornaments. Teller spent years in searching the area, and when his body was found after he had been missing for a time, a sack of ore rich in silver was resting beside it. It was thought that Teller had been killed near the cave of silver by another man who had trailed Teller, and was himself killed in the shoot-out. Repeated searches in the area where Teller's body was found, which has many caves, revealed nothing. It is now thought that the entrance

ARIZONA

to the cave of silver has been closed by an earthquake or cloudburst.

Coconino County—In 1582, Antonio de Espejo, an adventure-loving Spaniard, led a small expedition into what is now New Mexico in search of three missionaries who had been abandoned by Spanish soldiers. At the same time, Espejo was also searching for precious metal. Educated as a mining engineer in Cordova, Spain, he had accumulated his wealth through successful mining ventures in Mexico, and he was now interested in running down rumors that large quantities of gold and silver existed in the Arizona country.

Espejo traveled as far north as Zuni, New Mexico, and then swung west into Arizona, going as far as the Bill Williams Fork west of Prescott. Here, it is recorded in his own journals, he found silver, samples of the the ore which he took to Mexico on his return journey.

This much is historical fact, but from this point on legend takes over.

It is said that a party of Espejo's men, unbeknown to him, found gold in what is now the south central part of Coconino County. They took samples of the ore, made location maps, and left Espejo to return to Mexico City. When the news reached certain church officials, a second party was sent north to verify the report. It returned to Mexico and reported the finding of the gold just where Espejo's men said it would be.

About 1720, a party of padres, accompanied by a number of Spanish soldiers and some 200 Opata Indians, journeyed to the region and constructed a small village. The Indians were employed as forced laborers. As they brought out the ore it was smelted into bars, some of which were transported to Mexico City and the remainder kept stored in or near the mine.

In 1760 the mine and village were mysteriously abandoned, and the Spanish never again returned to it. Where was it located? The historian Bancroft thought it to be near Bill Williams Mountain south of Williams. Some place it in the Santa Maria Mountains near where Walnut Creek flows into Chino Creek. Still others believe the Spanish mine was located in Sycamore Canyon.

Coconino County—While a prisoner in Fort Sill, Oklahoma, in 1886, the Indian chief Geronimo offered to exchange his knowledge of certain gold deposits for his freedom. He had tricked the military so many times that the acceptance of his offer could not be considered. Furthermore, the army had no stomach for meeting his warriors in the mountain passes again. Some have tried to establish that he actually made a deal with certain officers at Fort Sill, but this seems unlikely. At least, he never secured his freedom.

It is said that Geronimo told a friend at Fort Sill that the Apaches' source of gold was in the Verde River country of Arizona. The vein was first found by the Apaches, according to Geronimo, and was later seized from them by a party of Spaniards passing through on their way to New

33

Mexico. Leaving part of their group behind to work the mine, the Spaniards erected an **arrastre** and a smelter for refining the ore.

Not being able to stand up to the Spaniards' weapons, the Indians waged a war of attrition. From the canyon walls in which the mine was located, the Apaches rolled boulders into the Spanish camp. They attacked from ambush when they were certain of success. They made frightening sounds at night and did everything they could to keep the Spanish miners in a constant state of turmoill. Nevertheless, the Spaniards refused to be driven away. They tunneled into the canyon wall where the ore became so rich that it could be taken directly to the smelter.

When a large number of gold bars had been smelted, it was planned to transport them to Mexico on mules and return with sufficient force to drive the Indians from the canyon. But when the pack train left the canyon, the Indians launched a furious attack, killing all of the Spaniards with the exception of two.

The two surviving miners waited their chance and returned to their camp where they hid the accumulation of gold bars in the mine tunnel and closed its entrance. At night they made their way out and finally reached Tubac, where they rested and then left on the long trip to Mexico City. Here they told the story of the lost Spanish mine in Sycamore Canyon and produced a map of its location.

The story of a gold mine in Sycamore Canyon was known to white men long before Geronimo offered to reveal its location in exchange for his freedom. Time and time again, signs of ancient mining activity in Sycamore Canyon were reported by hunters. Then, in 1853, a prospector named Clifford Haines fled into the upper reaches of the canyon when attacked by a party of Apaches. Exploring about after eluding his pursuers, he came upon what appeared to be the remains of an old Spanish mining village— ruins of some old stone houses, an **arrastre**, and broken parts of two-wheeled carts known as **carretas**. Scattered about were a few pieces of ore that Haines recognized as gold-bearing, and some broken mining tools. Fearing the Indians would discover him, he quickly made a map of the area and cautiously worked his way out of the canyon.

Haines tried to interest others in returning to the mine site with him, but found no one willing to enter the country dominated by hostile Indians. Finally he abandoned the idea and the map somehow fell into the hands of John T. Squires. Successful in organizing a party of miners, and armed with the Haines map, Squires led the group into Sycamore Canyon. They had no trouble in locating the old mining camp. They discovered a small cave in the canyon wall near the wreckage of the old mine. It contained more mining tools, several rotted sacks of mined ore, and rusted weapons of Spanish origin.

Squires and his men worked the mine one summer and packed their ore to Santa Fe, New Mexico, where it was smelted. One day they were attacked by a band of roving Apaches, and only a few of the men escaped to

Tucson to tell the story. As they fled the area, they saw the Indians setting about to destroy every trace of the mine site. It was not long after this that Squires was killed in a saloon fight.

After the Apaches withdrew from the area about 1886, some of the original members of the Squires party returned to Sycamore Canyon and made an extensive search for the mine but failed to find it. In 1896, William O. "Bearhunter" Howard, a game hunter for construction crews working on the Santa Fe Railroad, is said to have accidentally stumbled upon the ruins of the old mine. Strangely enough, he did not attempt to return to the site until a year or more later, when he led a party into the area in search of it. When nothing was found, the party broke up in disgust. Persisting in the search, Howard later reported that he had again found the mine, but he had no believers. Apparently he never attempted to work the mine and died a few years later.

Searches are still made for the old Spanish mine in Sycamore Canyon, and occasionally it is reported to have been found, but these reports have heretofore turned out to be nothing more than rumors.

There are two Sycamore Canyons in Arizona. One has its mouth at the Verde River northwest of Clarkdale, and extends for about 50 miles northeast, about half of its length being in Yavapai County and the remainder in Coconino County. The second Sycamore Canyon also has its mouth at the Verde River just north of its junction with the Gila, and extends northeastward to Mt. Ord, its entire length being in Maricopa County. The old Spanish gold mine is located in the super reaches of the Yavapai-Coconino County Sycamore Canyon.

Gila County—Felix (Francis Xavier) Aubrey had many hair-raising adventures on the plains of the early west, but is best remembered as the little Frenchman who wagered $1,000 that he could ride horseback from Santa Fe, New Mexico, to Independence, Missouri, in eight days. He made it in three days less than that time, killing several horses en route.

On another occasion, Aubrey was camped with a party of men in the Coyotero Apache country close to the Mogollon Rim in the Tonto Basin, when a small group of stray Apaches appeared. They wanted to trade for food, tobacco and clothing and they had a supply of gold nuggets to offer in exchange. Aubrey later wrote in his journal that they received $1,500 in gold for some castoff rags.

When pressed to reveal the source of their gold, the Indians only pointed toward the Mogollon Rim and made signs indicating that it was picked up on the surface of the ground. But aware that the gold taken from their placer deposits had real trading value, the Indians refused to give any further information.

The meeting of Aubrey and the Indians is believed to have taken place in the area of Pine (State 87), which lies just to the south of the Mogollon Rim.

Gila County—A small party of Pima Indians, returning to their reservation near the northern slopes of the Superstition Mountains after escorting a group of eastern hunters to the Mazatal Range, came upon the skeletons of two men, bleached white by the sun and scattered by predatory animals. Nearby the Indians found a shallow mining shaft, mining tools, utensils and a small pile of ore which the Indians saw to be generously sprinkled with gold. They picked up a few of the larger pieces to take with them.

Skirting the western side of the Superstitions, they made camp at the northern end of the Santa Ana (San Tan) Mountains. Later that evening an old prospector stopped at the Indians' camp, filled his water containers at the waterhole, and settled down for a chat. Noting the gold-bearing rocks, the prospector examined one and immediately saw that it was rich in gold. But not wanting to arouse the Indians, he played it down, saying that it had no value.

That night the prospector camped a short distance away, and in the morning he saw the Indians break camp and ride away. He returned to their campsite, and as he had hoped, they had left a few pieces of the ore behind. He examined the rocks thoroughly and verified his earlier opinion. Aware that the Indians had come from Mt. Ord, he set out to backtrack them. This he found not difficult until he came to the high rocky country north of the Superstitions. There all signs were lost in the boulders and he had to give up.

In Phoenix the ore he had kept assayed $35,000 to the ton. Telling no one where he had secured the ore, he soon returnd to the area and continued his search. Most of the remainder of his life he maintained the search without success, consistently believing the two skeletons marked the site of a rich mine somewhere around the base of Mt. Ord.

There are two Mt. Ords in Arizona. This story refers to the Mt. Ord on the Gila-Maricopa County line northeast of Phoenix.

Gila County—In 1871 a prospector named Miner reported the finding of a placer deposit in which one shovel full of earth panned out 17 ounces of gold. Not being able to find his way back to the site, he reported it as being in the vicinity of a butte that looked like a hat. This was presumed to be Sombrero Butte, north of the Salt River and between Cherry Creek and Canyon Creek.

The news touched off one of the greatest searches for a lost mine in the history of Arizona. At one time almost 300 men were scouring the wide area in which Miner led them, and the Governor of Arizona Territory even left his official duties to lead one of the parties.

From the very start, Miner seemed to have had only a hazy idea where his placer mine was located, but the searchers blindly followed him. After prospecting up the San Pedro to the mouth of the San Carlos, up that stream to its head, and thence to the Salt River, the men spread out into Tonto Basin to the mouth of Cherry Creek and into the slopes of the Sierra Anchas. Still they could not find the right hat-shaped butte that Miner insisted was his principal landmark. In utter disgust the searchers finally gave up and returned to their homes, denouncing Miner as a liar. There is still speculation that Miner's Lost Mine actually exists.

Gila County—Sometime around 1872, a soldier named Sanders was stationed at Fort Apache, Arizona. Detailed to scout a band of Indians suspected of stealing some cattle from a Salt River ranch, he led his troops toward the Sierra Anchas. At this point he dispatched his troops on another mission and proceeded on alone.

After skirting around the eastern end of the Anchas, he came to Coon Creek and traveled its bed, now almost dry. About 10 miles from its head he came to a waterfall which obstructed his progress. Leading his horse, he picked his way up a steep incline to the crest of a ridge and sat down to rest.

Like other soldiers, Sanders was usually on the lookout for gold and silver deposits. He noted that the rock he was seated on was a large block of quartz, and that the entire ridge was actually a quartz dike. He examined the rock and found that it was rich in gold. Suspecting that the ledge was part of the mother lode, he proved it to himself by picking up rock after rock in the vicinity—all rich in gold. Unable to believe his good luck, he packed all the rocks he could carry and continued on his journey, careful to observe the country closely for landmarks.

Back at Fort Apache, Sanders tried to obtain a discharge, but was told that he would have to serve out the remainder of his enlistment, about two years. His discharge finally came through just as expeditions were preparing to take to the field in search of Miner's lost mine. Fearing that they might be searching for the quartz dike he had found, he joined the parties and traveled with them to the Sierra Anchas. When they came to a point near the head of Coon Creek, Sanders was certain that someone in the spread-out party would stumble upon his find.

However, while in this area, one of the party was injured by a falling rock and the whole group moved on to a better camp at Oak Springs. Sanders watched his chance and found an opportunity to sneak away. He found his ledge again and gathered more ore specimens. When the Miner party moved out of the area, Sanders went to Phoenix where he showed the specimens to several men, but revealed nothing about the source of the ore.

Some six months after the Miner party disbanded, Sanders left Phoenix for Fort McDowell with three other men. At old Camp Reno they met a party of soldiers who warned them to turn back because of a band of Indians on the warpath. Two members of the group heeded the advise, but Sanders and a lone companion proceeded on. Neither was ever seen alive again. About three weeks after their disappearance became known, a search party left Phoenix and trailed the two men to Walnut Springs in the western slopes of the Sierra Anchas. Here the trail was completely lost and the party gave up.

Years later two cattlemen were riding down Coon Creek when they came upon a human skull. In searching for the rest of the skeleton they found two partially buried skeletons which they took to be those of white men. Nearby they located the ruins of a cabin amid ashes. Obviously the cabin had been fired by Indians who had killed the white men.

In digging a grave for the remains of the two men, the cattlemen uncovered a rock that contained gold. This they took back to Phoenix with them and cleaned it of its crust of dirt. One side appeared to have been cut or ground with a hard substance, and one of the other sides presented a perfect surface of gold on which had been carved with a knife the word SANDERS.

Without knowing it, the cattlemen had stumbled upon the long lost Sanders mine. Neither they, nor anybody else, ever found it again.

Gila County—The Tonto Apaches were a renegade band under the leadership of Chief Del Shay (or Del Shea, meaning "red ant"). They more or less made their permanent home in Tonto Basin, a triangular area of wild, striking beauty, 3,000 feet below and formed by the Mogollon Rim, the Mazatal Range and the Sierra Ancha Mountains. They were long known to be in the possession of gold deposits because they frequently came in from their haunts with rich pieces of gold ore and nuggets to exchange for merchandise in the military posts and frontier settlements. One old Apache is said to have described the gold as coming from a vein of white quartz taken from an eight-ft. hole covered by a packrat nest.

Camp Reno, an outpost of Fort McDowell, was established at the foot of Reno Pass to help contain the Tonto Apaches. Soldiers stationed at Fort McDowell frequently suffered from gold fever due to the many stories they heard of Apache gold existing almost under their noses. However, they were generally kept too busy chasing Apaches to do any serious prospecting. Upon being discharged, many of them took to the hills as prospectors—and some of them fell victims to Apache cunning.

Camp Reno was abandoned in 1870 and the troops stationed there were transferred to Fort McDowell. On their way to the new garrison they met two recently discharged soldiers still in their army uniforms. They carried rifles and an ample supply of provisions, and they said they were headed for the Mt. Ord country to search for the rumored gold source of the Tonto Apaches. They were warned of the danger ahead of them and urged to turn back. Determined, however, they proceeded on their way and were never heard of again.

About five years later two sheepherders came upon five male skeletons scattered over the rocky northern slopes of Mt. Ord. Two of the dead men were judged to be white and the remainder were thought to be Indians. On the frames of the white men were remnants of army uniforms. Empty cartridge shells and two army rifles were found nearby. In the pack of one of the men was found pieces of white quartz sprinkled with gold.

It is believed that the two soldiers had found the source of the Tonto

Apaches' gold and were on their way out of the mountains when attacked by the Indians. It is said that the many searches for the soldiers' lost mine have all failed.

Graham County—There are legends of "mountains of silver" and "mountains of gold" in several of the western states, and two in Arizona—one in the north and one in the south. This story concerns a Mexican named Pedro Encinas, who, as a captive of the Apaches in Northeastern Arizona, was aware that the Indians gathered silver from the slopes of a mountain where it lay in plentiful supply. Although Encinas was forced to help gather the silver on occasions, he was not certain of the mountain's exact location, but he believed it to be a peak in the Gila Mountains—possibly Gila Peak —north of the town of Fort Thomas (US 70).

After Pedro Encinas escaped from the Indians, he made his way back to Mexico and organized an expedition to locate the mountain of silver. He was armed with a letter from the governor of Sonora addressed to the acting Indian Agent for the San Carlos Reservation, on whose lands the mountain was thought to be located. The letter asked his cooperation in granting the Mexicans permission to explore the area. This permission was granted, but the stipulation was made that if any silver was found on reservation lands, it was not to be mined.

L. K. Thompson of Salt River Valley, a brother-in-law of Pedro Encinas, accompanied the expedition and later reported that the source of Apache silver had indeed been found. But when it was determined that the silver was located on the San Carlos Reservation, the party abandoned the project. At the request of the Indian Agent all members of the party took an oath not to reveal the location of the "mountain of silver" until permission to work the mine could be secured. This permission was never granted, and one by one, the members of the search party died off.

Graham County—The Old Mansfield Trail ran from the San Francisco River in Catron County, New Mexico, to the headwaters of Eagle Creek in Graham County, Arizona. It was more of a mule path than a trail and hardly any traces of it can be found today. But "Old Man" Mansfield, a prospector of whom very little is known, operated a mine, now also lost, and packed his ore out over this path. It was a region of wild Apache bands and many a prospector, including Mansfield, fell victim of Apache ferocity.

In 1862 a party of three prospectors were picking their way along the old trail when they came upon a lone black burro idly grazing a short distance away. It was wearing a packsaddle that appeared to be rather new, and lashed to each side was a large rawhide sack that seemed to be heavily loaded. Believing its owner to be in the area, they shouted, but received no reply. They searched the area, but found no sign of human life. After waiting a few hours, thinking the burro's owner would return, they investigated the sacks and found them loaded with gold ore which they described as being of "incredible richness."

The prospectors camped at the spot that night, but by morning, when the mule's owner did not appear they concluded that some mishap had befallen him. Adding the loaded burro to their own train, they moved on, certain that somewhere in the area was a gold mine of fabulous richness, its owner probably killed by Apaches.

Nearing the Arizona end of the Old Mansfield Trail, the party of three prospectors were themselves attacked by Indians. Two of the men were killed, but the third managed to escape unseen into the bushes and hide out until the Indians left the scene. The lone survivor eventually reached a small Mexican settlement where he told the story. In later years many men searched for the mine which became known as the Lost Black Burro Mine. So far as it is known, it has never been found. Most of the searches have been concentrated in the area of the junction of San Francisco and Blue rivers north of Clifton.

Maricopa County—When John Carroll operated a trading post at Fort McDowell, on the west bank of the Verde River near its junction with the Salt River, most of his trade was with soldiers stationed at the post. The income of a soldier in those days was meager, but one unnamed soldier usually had plenty of gold nuggets to pay for his purchases. When his supply of gold ran low, Carroll gladly extended him credit for the trooper always came in later and paid up.

When Fort McDowell was abandoned as a military post and the soldiers were about to be transferred elsewhere, Carroll asked the soldier-creditor to pay up his account. The soldier pleaded that he had a source of gold, but did not have the time to get it before leaving with his outfit. When the storekeeper insisted that the bill must be paid, the soldier offered to reveal the secret location of his gold in exchange for a bill marked "paid in full." This was more than agreeable with Carroll.

Escorting Carroll to the flagpole on the parade ground, the soldier instructed the storekeeper to sight directly on Weaver's Needle, visible in the distance to the south. "The secret mine," said the soldier, "will be found on the extension of this imaginary line, just beyond and across the first main canyon." With these words the soldier's bill was erased.

John Carroll sold his trading post and spent many years in searching for the soldier's secret mine, but never found it. He finally concluded that he had been taken in by the soldier, who indeed had a source of gold, but had simply given Carroll false directions to it. Old prospectors said that Carroll was the biggest fool on the frontier for taking a soldier's word for anything, but Carroll noted that they, too, searched for the lost mine.

Maricopa County—Sometime in the late 1880's, an Indian cowhand known as Yaqui Valentino was riding the range in the Four Peaks area northeast of Phoenix. While engaged in chasing a black maverick calf through the thick scrub, he threw his rope as the critter entered an open space. As the struggling animal threshed around, it uncovered a rock which the cowboy recognized as having gold content. He placed the rock in his pocket and was about to proceed with his work when his horse broke through some half-rotted timbers revealing a shallow pit which the cowboy took to be the entrance to an old mine shaft. Investigating further, the cowboy came upon the half-covered foundations of an old cabin. He poked through the ruins and uncovered enough tools to lead him to believe that Mexicans or Spaniards had once occupied the place as they worked the mine.

Back at his camp that night, Yaqui Valentino related his experience, but refused to tell exactly where he had picked up the gold-bearing rock which he displayed. There was considerable excitement in the camp at the prospect of finding an old gold mine, and some anger that Valentino remained tight-lipped. When an Indian friend later told Valentino that the cowboys planned to kill him if he did not let them in on the secret, he quietly left his job and went to work for another outfit near Rye, almost due south of the Four Peaks.

One day Valentino told Henry Hardt, an American with whom he was on friendly terms, about the mine and offered him a one-third interest for assisting in its development. Hardt agreed, but when the time came to go to the site, Valentino begged off, saying that he had had a frightful dream in which they were attacked and killed by Apaches. Reluctantly, however, he finally agreed to take Hardt part way to the mine. Upon reaching the western foothills of the Four Peaks, the Indian refused to go a step farther. No persuasion by Hardt would move him. Hardt believed the mine was nearby, but he was never able to find it.

A few months later Valentino was dead of natural causes, and the secret of the Black Maverick Lost Mine was sealed.

Maricopa County—Early on the morning of Febraury 2, 1890, the huge Walnut Grove Dam on the Hassayampa River 40 miles above Wickenburg, burst with a deafening roar and within an hour swept away a second and smaller dam as if it had not been there.

It had been feared that the dam might not be able to contain its rain-swollen waters, and when it became obvious that the dam would go, a rider was sent to warn the people below. His first stop was at a construction camp saloon about 15 miles below the dam. The reveling crowd here was too hilariously drunk to heed the warning and laughed at the rider. Soon, he, too, was drunk.

The loss of life in the flood was never established, but 83 bodies were later recovered, some as many as 25 years later, when their skeletons were found in the desert sands along the Hassayampa's receded banks. In the Congress Store at Seymour, $1,500 had been hidden in the rafters of the building. This was swept away as well as $5,000 in gold kept in a heavy iron safe in Bob Brow's Saloon at Fool's Gulch. How many other small treasures were carried away by the raging waters will never be known. Below the broken dam the Hassayampa was over its normal banks for miles. It is believed that the heavy safe would not have carried very far, and that it is now probably covered with desert sand. Many searchers have failed to find it.

Maricopa County—Along US 60 about four miles west of Wickenburg is a plaque marking the site of what is known as the Wickenburg Massacre, a stage holdup which took place November 5, 1871, in which the driver and five passengers were killed. Although the holdup men were dressed as Indians, there was a strong opinion at the time that the outlaws were white men in disguise. The point has never been established. It is believed that between $40,000 and $100,000 was taken from the mails and the passengers, and those who believed that the crime was committed by Indians argued that they would not have taken the treasure far, but would have buried it nearby. Whether or not there is any treasure buried near the massacre site, many searches of the area have been made.

Maricopa County—In 1878 two prospectors completed a hazardous journey from the west coast of Mexico to the Estrella Mountains southwest of Phoenix. After they had sufficiently recovered from the rigors of their trip, they made their way high into the rock-ribbed canyons and started their search for gold. They found it—plenty of it.

For several months they worked long hours taking out as much gold as possible before Indians, who infested the area, discovered their presence. They estimated they had cached away $50,000 worth of gold before a band of Pimas found them and ordered them to move out. They could take the accumulated gold with them, the Indians said, but they must be out of the mountains in three days.

Such a command was taken by the two Mexican prospectors to indicate a sign of weakness. They elected to ignore it and continued their mining operations. At the end of the allotted time, the Pimas returned. Without warning they opened fire on the miners, killing one. The second, badly wounded, managed to escape.

The injured man finally reached Tucson, where he was hospitalized. He had no further interest in the mine, he said, and he would gladly turn it over to any party of men who would give him safe escort to the spot in order that he could recover the $50,000.

In due time a party was organized. On the day they were scheduled to to leave for the Estrellas, the Mexican was found dead on the streets of Tucson. So far as it is known the mine and the $50,000 were never found.

Maricopa County—Colby Thomas, a mining engineer, was 86 years of age when Iretaba, an aged Apache, told him of a mine he had visited as a boy and had taken out a quantity of gold. Iretaba gave Thomas detailed directions to the mine, which he said was located 20 feet southwest of a large palo verde tree on a high mesa overlooking a wash a few miles northwest of Hughes Well. Its entrance, he said, was covered with a large flat rock.

According to Iretaba, who was sometimes known as Puncher Bob, two white men had come to Tucson in the 1850's and prospected in the Four Peak area. They found a blowout loaded with gold. After taking out some of the rich ore, they became frightened by the prospect of an Indian attack, loaded the ore on their burros, carefully concealed the entrance to the mine, and returned to Tucson.

In the absence of the two prospectors, the Indians discovered that the mine had been worked. When the miners regained their courage and returned to the site, they were ambushed and killed. According to Iretaba, his father had been a member of the slaying party.

Despite his advanced age and a condition of near blindness, Colby Thomas made a trip to the region of the mine alone. He located the wash and the bench above it, but instead of finding one palo verde tree that stood out from the others, they all looked alike to him. Short of provisions and water, he returned to Tucson and again consulted with Iretaba. The old Apache thought Thomas had found the right area, but had failed to locate the right tree.

After the strenuous trip Thomas became ill and it was several months before he could renew the search. This time he did not attempt to make the trip alone, but took along a partner named Edward Abbott. When they reached the wash, Thomas remained in camp while Abbott scoured the region for a large palo verde tree near a flat rock. The trip was a failure and they returned to Tucson to seek Iretaba's advice again. The Indian had disappeared and was never found. Neither was the mine.

Maricopa County—A section of State 69-Interstate 17 north of Phoenix is known as the Woolsey Trail after King S. Woolsey, Arizona pioneer and veteran Indian fighter. About 30 miles east of New River (State 69), in what was known then, as now, as the Camp Creek country, Woolsey and a party of Indian hunters made camp at a place known locally as Squaw Hollow. Things were quiet and someone suggested that this was good country in which to prospect. On the following day the men fanned out through the mesquite-covered hills to do that.

According to Judge John T. Alsop, well-known Arizona pioneer who was with the party but remained in the camp, it was not long before some of the men brought in a hat full of what he described as the richest gold ore he had ever seen. It had been broken from a ledge, and the men finding it reported that a great quantity of the ore was exposed. Judge Alsop did not know exactly where the ore had been found, nor did he later visit the spot because of subsequent events.

Excitement in the camp was high, but before any of the men could return to the ledge of gold, Apaches attacked in overwhelming numbers and the party had to leave the area in a hurry. During the following months the men of the party became separated, and Apaches in the area of the ledge made it too dangerous for anyone to return. Knowledge of the ledge was kept a secret among the men, who planned to mine the lode legally when conditions permitted. However, only a few of the men ever returned to Squaw Hollow. One of these was Judge Alsop. Headquartering at Camp Creek, he spent many weeks prospecting the region, but failed to locate any sign of the ledge. He expressed surprise that he found no indication that any of the original party had ever returned to the area. Camp Creek can be located on a quad map. It rises at Maverick Butte near the Ashdale Ranger Station and flows southeast into the Verde River at Needle Rock, a popular Phoenix recreational area.

Years later, a sheepherder passing through the Camp Creek region claimed to have come across a man who had built a cabin in the area and was working a rich gold mine nearby. The sheepherder said the miner was bringing the ore out on burros, grinding it in a large iron mortar and washing the gold out in the creek. When the sheepherder returned to the area a few years later, he found the cabin in ruins. He searched for the mine but failed to find it.

The area around Squaw Hollow is known to be highly mineralized. It is also an area where any search would literally have to be made "on hands and knees," as one prospector said. If this mine hasn't been found and worked out, it is this writer's opinion that it is still there in Squaw Hollow.

Maricopa County—Palmer C. Ashley was helping his father work a low-grade prospect in Morgan City Wash, north of US 60-89 and some place between the towns of Wittman and Morristown. The year was 1934. One day when his father was away on business in Phoenix, young Ashley decided to take a hike. As he was making his way up Morgan City Wash, he kept his eyes on the lookout for a high fluted wall an old prospector had told him about. Slipping on a rock, he fell and suffered some slight bruises. As he sat there catching his breath, he noted a ledge of white quartz streaked with red and green colorations. He chipped off a piece and placed it in his pack, having no idea of its value, but admiring its color.

Weeks later, when his father examined the samples in his son's pack, he recognized the rock's rich gold content. Father and son searched for the ledge in Morgan Wash and its many side canyons, but were never able to locate the ledge.

Maricopa County—In 1878, a prospector named Cal Madden came into Wickenburg from a trip into the Vulture Mountains, famed as the scene of Henry Wickenburg's rich Vulture Mine. He had with him specimens of rich

ARIZONA

gold ore which he claimed to have taken from a large white quartz blowout not many miles from the Vulture Mine. Madden's appearance caused a great deal of local excitement, but he refused to reveal any information as to where he had found the ore other than that it was in the Vultures. After purchasing supplies and equipment, he slipped out of Wickenburg at night, careful to see that no one followed him.

When Madden did not return after several weeks, a search party went out to look for him. The worst fears of his friends were realized when his stripped and mutilated body was found not far from rugged Vulture Peak, due south of Wickenburg and about six miles from the Hassayampa River. It was speculated that he had been surprised and killed by Indians before he had reached his blowout.

Subsequent searches for Madden's mine produced nothing but failures, until about 20 years later when a Mexican prospector, wandering about in the mountains a few miles west of Vulture Creek, came upon a blowout of white quartz which showed some signs of ancient work. It was thought at the time that this was the Madden mine, for the description of the area and the color of the quartz matched the information Madden had revealed. But the mine showed evidence of having been worked long before Madden's appearance in the region. Nor did the blowout produce the rich ore to match Madden's samples. It was finally concluded that this was not Madden's lost mine. Presumably, it is still there.

Maricopa County—About 1858, two Frenchmen appeared in Phoenix, and after outfitting themselves, announced that they were going into the Estrella Mountains to the southwest in search of a lost Spanish mine. Many searches have been made for mines in this area once worked by the Spanish, and there is plenty of evidence that the Spanish were active in the Estrellas.

Within a few weeks the unnamed pair of Frenchmen were back in Phoenix with a quantity of rich silver ore to sell. All they would say was that they had found it just where they thought it would be. Without elaborating on this, they left again. Upon their return to Phoenix, they again had silver ore to sell. From their next trip to the Estrellas, they never returned, nor was their fate ever learned. If, indeed, they had found a lost Spanish mine, it is still lost.

Maricopa County—Jacob Walz, of the Lost Dutchman Mine fame, never tried to conceal the fact that he had a secret gold mine in the Superstition Mountains. He talked about it freely, and showed samples of the ore taken from it. He also successfully evaded all those who tried to follow him to his mine. Perhaps he killed some of them.

One of those who heard of the Lost Dutchman's Mine from Walz's own lips was a Phoenix shoemaker, an old German named Rodig or Rohrdik. After Walz's death, the shoemaker decided to find the Dutchman's mine—or, if not that, a better one. He began making periodic trips into the Superstitions, always returning empty-handed. Eventually his funds were depleted, and his little business vanished from neglect. Still he persisted, and his searches began taking him in ever widening circles around the Superstitions.

One day Rodig camped in the Four Peaks area, a group of rocky heights in the southern part of the Mazatal Mountains. Looking down at the black sand along a canyon floor, he detected signs of color. Digging into the sand, he found it to be rich in gold dust and nuggets, but he had barely panned out the first two shovelfuls when shouts resounded from the canyon walls. He looked up to see a band of Apaches rushing toward him.

Rodig managed somehow to escape from the Indians, but he was never able to relocate the placer. Several years later he was observed by two cowboys to be wandering around in a seemingly dazed condition. Eventually he disappeared and his fate is unknown. He had failed to find the Dutchman's lost mine, but he had found—and lost—his own.

Maricopa County—In a fork formed by Arizona 85 and a dirt road to the east, south of Gila Bend and between the Sand Tank Mountains on the east and the north end of the Sauceda Mountains on the west, is a hat-shaped peak once known as Sierra Sombrero, but now commonly known as Hat Mountain. Standing about six miles east of State 85, its summit rises high enough above the surrounding hills so that its distinctive shape can be seen for miles in all directions. Near this peak is a lost tungsten mine that should make its finder rich.

John "Cap" Linger was an old prospector who worked in the great copper mine at Ajo, Arizona, but his heart was never in it. Switching from a burro to a Model-T Ford during World War I, he prospected the hills whenever he found the chance. After working the Pozo Redondo Range west of Ajo, he started north, prospecting as he went in the hills and canyons of the Sauceda Mountains and eventually into the region around Hat Mountain.

One day he returned to his home in Ajo and excitedly told his wife that he had found a rich tungsten lode. To prove it, he showed her some heavy rocks, but she had to take his word for it that they were rich in tungsten, then in great shortage. He drew her a detailed map of the location in the event anything happened to him while he tried to raise the capital to develop the find.

Mrs. Linger knew less than nothing about ores and mining, but she dutifully tucked the map away in a place that only a woman can think of. With the close of the war in Europe, the bottom dropped out of the copper market, and Linger was let out of his job, a job he had no stomach for anyway.

But there was a living to be made, and it was no time to try to raise money for a mining operation. In search of work, the Lingers packed up and moved back east where Cap soon came down with pneumonia and died. Mrs. Linger still had the heavy rocks Cap had persisted in dragging with them. She took them with her when she moved back to Ajo to live with relatives.

She was there when World War II broke out, and reading of the critical demand for tungsten, she recalled her husband's find near Hat Mountain. She showed the rocks to some mining men and asked if they were worth anything. Were they? High grade tungsten, she was told, was worth more than gold!

Mrs. Linger searched for and found Cap's map stuffed away among some odds and ends all those years. A party was organized, and after searching the Hat Mountain region for several weeks, returned to report that it had only succeeded in becoming thoroughly lost. Cap's map could not be deciphered. Cap Linger's lost tungsten lode is still lost.

Mohave County—A lone man dressed as a soldier waited on the upper end of Cottonwood Island in the middle of the Colorado River, about 30 miles north of what is now Needles, California. The year was 1880. He carried a Henry rifle, and across the river on the Arizona side he had two horses tethered in the bushes. As the steamer Gila appeared on its downstream journey to Yuma, he signaled as if in distress. Capt. Jack Mellon of the Gila ordered the wheel reversed and sent his first mate and two Indians in a skiff to bring the man aboard.

Earlier that morning the Gila had taken on board a half ton of silver bars and 300 ounces of gold at the silver mining camp of El Dorado Canyon. The gold rested in a small safe in the captain's cabin, but the silver bullion was stacked on the deck of the steamer. The soldier ordered the captain to surrender the strongbox, which was done after some delay, and the two Indians, under rifle point, placed it in the skiff. Then the Indians were ordered to load the silver bars on the skiff. After a few hundred pounds were placed aboard the small boat, the man in uniform ordered it stopped, seeing that the skiff was becoming overloaded. The pirate then leaped into the skiff, and with a warning wave of his rifle, shoved off for the Arizona bank of the Colorado.

When the Gila reached Hardyville that afternoon, a posse was organized and set out for Cottonwood Island. When the men returned a few days later, they reported having found the tracks of two horses leading away from the river bank where the abandoned skiff was located. But the tracks were lost on the high ridge above the river. Reaching Crossman Spring, the party had come upon a horse that had recently been shot, apparently because it had a broken leg. Here they found traces of a camp, upon learning that a man believed to have been the pirate dressed as a soldier had passed through here four days earlier, the search was abandoned.

People who had seen the traveler reported that he appeared to be traveling light. It was assumed, therefore, that he was carrying only the gold with him, and that the silver bullion had been buried near Crossman Spring (later known as Crescent Spring), where his second horse had become disabled. A party immediately went out in search of the silver, but found only the dead horse.

About 1900, a miner found a single bar of silver while digging a well a few hundred feet north of the spring. This event touched off another search for the silver, but again nothing was found. Since it was known for certain that several bars had been taken from the Gila, it was presumed that this was a stray from the larger cache nearby.

The little camp of Crossman's (Crescent) Spring is a total ghost today, its exact site completely lost, but some painstaking research could doubtless reveal its location. As to the authenticity of the story, it is a matter of public record, having been headlined in local area newspapers at the time.

Mohave County—This is one of the very, very few buried treasure stories that can be pinpointed to a precise spot—and it is easily located. To some treasure hunters it will not have the appeal of gold and silver. To others it will have more. The prize is books and whiskey! The location? Latitude 30° 00′ 24″, Longitude 114° 34′ 40″—and these are official.

Camp Mojave was announced as a military reservation on August 4, 1870, although there had been a military post here for many years during the Indian troubles. Prior to the outbreak of the Civil War, Companies F and I, 6th United States Infantry, were garrisoned here. It was considered the hottest and most undesirable of all U. S. military outposts. No tears were shed when the troops were withdrawn from here in 1861.

Peter R. Brady, long a resident of Florence, Arizona, was in the employ of the Army at Fort Mojave at the time of its abandonment in 1861. When the soldiers marched away, he was left behind to destroy anything of value so that it would not fall into the hands of hostile Indians. He was also under orders to fire some of the buildings. As the troops disappeared into the desert hills, Brady prepared to carry out his assignment. He looked about. Little had been left behind. But what was this? The post had abandoned its entire library! In his own words, Brady later described it as a "good library."

Not wishing to destroy the books, Brady dug a deep hole under the floor of the commissary building. He carefully wrapped the books in tarpaulins and placed them in the pit. He now looked about for additional valuables and found two barrels of whiskey and several cases of what he described as "excellent wines." He enlarged the hole to accommodate the spirits. When all was in place he covered the pit with the removed dirt.

Brady stated that he then set fire to the commissary building, and waited until it was reduced to a coat of ashes that covered the secret cache "to thwart the hands of inquisitive Indians." He stated many times before his death that he believed the books and the whiskey were still where he had buried them.

The old buildings of Fort Mojave have now completely disappeared, but the forms of their foundations can still be traced. The writer has secured an engineers map of the old fort clearly showing the layout of the structures.

ARIZONA

This is available to anyone through the National Archives and Record Service, Washington 25, D. C.

Permission to explore and dig in the area must be secured through the U. S. Department of the Interior, Bureau of Indian Affairs, Phoenix Area Office, P. O. Box 7007, Phoenix, Arizona. The area is now an Indian Reservation, and permission must also be secured from the Needles Indian Colony Tribal Council, 521 Merriam Street, Needles, California. It has been the writer's experience that such permission, if any, will be granted only under the strictest of supervisory conditions. The fort site is almost directly across the Colorado River from Needles.

Mohave County—In 1942, two brothers from Los Angeles traced down some very rich float gold ore to its source in the upper reaches of the Cerbat Mountains north of the ghost town of Chloride. They returned to Kingman for explosives and other supplies, and when they left they were accompanied by a woman. After blasting out two sacks full of the ore, they carefully concealed all signs of their activity and took it to Los Angeles, where it was assayed by a friend. It proved to be very rich in gold content.

About this time the two brothers were inducted into the army. Eventually they were sent to the Pacific islands where both were killed in action. When the assayer friend learned of their deaths, he looked up the woman who had seen the mine, and together they went into the Cerbat Mountains to stake out a claim. They arrived at what she thought was the right place, but they found no ore and no signs of any blasting activity. After spending several days scouring the area, they gave up. The mine has never been found, and it is believed that the site has been covered by a cloudburst.

Mohave County—In 1894, a prospector named Sam Whitlesy found a ledge of gold that assayed $35,000 to the ton. He told friends that the ledge was located within two miles of Sitgreaves Pass in the Black Mountains near the ghost town of Oatman. In a fight with two men attempting to follow him to the mine, Whitlesy killed them, but was himself so badly wounded that he later died. A great deal of futile searching has been made for this lost mine, which is located in one of Arizona's largest gold producing areas.

Navajo County—In 1885, Mark Carpenter made a rich silver strike on Silver Creek in the area of Shumway. He loaded his saddlebags with samples of the ore and was headed for St. John when he was attacked by Apaches who took his provisions and galloped away, taking his horse but leaving the loaded burro. Badly wounded, Carpenter managed to mount the burro and ride on. Sometime later he was found by a party of soldiers. Taken to the nearest army camp, Carpenter soon died of his wounds. Many people, including some of the soldiers, later searched the Silver Creek area for Carpenter's mine, but it was never found.

Navajo County—In the summer of 1855 a prospector named Darlington and his family were returning to Illinois from the California gold fields where he had struck it rich. In the party was his wife Althea, his young son and seven men who had joined the party along its route of travel, considering it safer to travel in numbers.

In one of the two Darlington wagons were sacks containing $300,000 in gold. When they reached the Sunset Crossing of the Little Colorado River, about six miles north of the present town of Winslow, Mrs. Darlington became ill and died. She was buried in a box built by the post trader at Sunset Crossing, and it was so heavy that it required six men to lower it into the shallow grave which Darlington himself filled in and leveled off to resemble the surrounding earth.

Years later it was learned that Darlington had placed half of his fortune —$150,000—in the coffin as his wife's share. While the site of the grave is today known by a few people, it is kept a secret to thwart grave robbers.

Navajo County—Navajo National Monument is within the boundaries of the Navajo Indian Reservation, and lies at the edge of an almost roadless area nearly 20 miles from a paved highway. According to Navajo legend, there is a cave high in the precipitous wall of a canyon near the cliff dwellings known as Inscription House. This cave is filled with a great quantity of turquoise which was sacred to the Navajo. It is believed that the turquoise was placed in the cave in the 13th century, and that its entrance was covered to conceal it. The exact location of the cave has been handed down from generation to generation, and it is believed that only three Indians knew the secret until recent years, when the concealed entrance to the cave collapsed, revealing the pile of precious turquoise from the canyon floor. This is truly a legend come true!

Pima County—Almost all Arizona missions have their stories of buried treasures and lost mines. San Xavier del Bac is no exception. The beautiful structure stands, brilliant in the desert sun, a few miles south of Tucson and two miles to the west of US 89, overlooking historic Santa Cruz Valley. Shortly after its founding by Jesuit Father Eusebio Francisco Kino in 1700 (at a different site), an old Papago Indian told him of a rich outcropping of silver in the Santa Catalina Mountains to the east. A few days later the faithful Papago led the priest to the site and Father Kino lost no time in developing and working the mine, which became known as the La Esmerelda (the Emerald), so named because of the greenish color of the ore. Before long gold was discovered in the area and more mines were opened.

Indian workers carried the rich ore in sacks on their backs to the arrastres constructed at the mission. Here the ore was smelted into bars and stamped with the mine code and mission symbol. Most of these bars were stored, but a few were used in making church ornaments. Early day miners who saw the interior of the mission estimated the value of these ornaments at $60,000.

Father Kino died in 1711 and the mission passed through many years of hardships from Indian revolts and Apache raids. In 1723 the Pima and Papago Indians jointly revolted and attacked San Xavier. Faithful neophytes dutifully carried all the stored bullion and church ornaments to the La Esmerelda Mine and buried them deep underground. Before the revolt of 1723 was over, the missions of San Xavier del Bac, Tumacacori and Guevavi were all partially destroyed and the padres abandoned them. It was eight years before they returned to remain in peaceful possession until another revolt in 1751 forced a second abandonment.

In 1754 the priests returned to San Xavier and this time the great treasure and church ornaments were brought down from the mountains and again stored at the mission. Only occasional Apache raids broke the peaceful and industrious activity of the Arizona missions. Then in 1767, the Jesuit padres were expelled from the New World. The vast treasure, now increased in value many times through the accumulated products of the mines, was carted across the valley to the mountains and once more concealed in the La Esmerelda Mine. There it remained until a year later when the Franciscan padres took over the missions. Once more the great treasure was returned to Mission San Xavier and there it remained until 1827.

In 1822 Mexico threw off the yoke of Spain. Five years later all priests on Mexican soil not native to the land were ordered to leave. When the Franciscans departed, not being able to take their vast treasure of gold and silver with them, it was hauled to the La Esmerelda Mine and buried once more. There, supposedly, it still remains. All efforts to locate the fabulous wealth stored within the La Esmerelda have failed. There are those who believe the story is based on pure legend, but others are just as certain that the treasure and the mine is there in the Santa Catalina Mountains.

Pima County—When Captain Juan Bautista de Anzac visited San Xavier del Bac Mission in 1775, he noted the violence of the Apaches in the region and ordered the small garrison stationed at Tubac to the south to be moved near Tucson to afford protection to the settlers, the padres and their charges. After the transfer had been accomplished, Father Francisco Tomas Garces built a new mission and named it San Jose del Tucson. Little is known of this mission's history because it was always overshadowed by the larger and more important San Xavier del Bac. San Jose del Tucson was eventually abandoned and all that remains of it today, one and one-half miles southwest of downtown Tucson, are some shapeless forms of crumbled adobe.

A. S. Reynolds, a pioneer who knew the mission and its gardens in the early days, was among those who told tales of treasure hunters digging in the old ruins in search of a treasure that was never defined. Only a single old Spanish coin is known to have been found.

Pima County—Some of the richest gold and silver mines ever found in North America were located near the southern Arizona missions, across the Mexican border in Sonora. Mines in this area are definitely known to have been worked by the Spanish, and some under the supervision of the mission padres. Less than 50 miles from Mission Tumacacori, now a national monument, a great deposit of silver was discovered in 1736, and several nuggets weighing a ton or more were found. It is claimed that one nugget weighed 4,000 pounds.

When the United States purchased the strip of land between the Gila River and the present boundary of Mexico, it was mainly because of our interest in the rich mining lands known to exist in the region. Walled in by these rich ore-producing mountains, and located in the very center of a mining region known from the earliest days, it seems likely that the mission padres had knowledge of the rich ores in the nearby mountains. But whether they engaged in any extensive mining activity is an unsettled point. Nevertheless, the stories of lost mission mines never cease.

The tower of Tumacacori Mission is said to have contained two tiny holes, one in the east wall and one in the west. By looking through the hole in the east wall it is said that one could spot the exact location on the faraway mountainside where the mission's treasure was hidden. That portion of the mission tower was in ruins when taken over by the National Park Service in 1908, so it is quite unlikely that anyone in modern times would have had the opportunity to investigate this interesting claim. If such a hole existed in the east wall of the tower, it would have peered into the Santa Rita Mountains, and the Santa Ritas are closely associated with the stories of the mission mines.

It is further claimed that markers indicated the trail from Tumacacori to a distant mine and the treasure site, and several people are reported to have found such markers from time to time. Quite likely most of these markers would have disappeared since they were placed there some 200 years ago. One marker found several years ago was in the form of a scallop shell, the mission's symbol, chiseled into an enormous boulder. An arrow pointed to the east, presumably in the direction of the mine.

Of the several mission lost mines, the one known as the Mine With the Iron Door, or the Escalante Mine, is one of the most famous. There are several versions of the story, but most agree that the entrance to the mine was through a strong door. Sometimes the door is of weathered oak fitted so expertly into a wall of solid rock that it could be detected only after the closest inspection of the canyon wall. It has been said, too, that the entrance to the mine was through a natural formation of iron deposits, hence the name "iron door."

In 1698 a party of Papago Indians hunting deer in the Santa Catalinas came across a rich outcropping of gold ore. They carried the news back to the padres at San Xavier del Bac. An investigation revealed the report to be true, and the responsibility for developing the mine was assigned to Father Silvestre Velez de Escalante. Indians packed the ore out of the mountains to a small camp where a chapel was established and an **arrastre** crushed the ore after which it was smelted into bars.

As it was several miles to the safety of the mission, and attacks by hostile Apaches were always a threat, Father Escalante ordered the Indian workers to prepare a secret room which was chiseled out of the hard rock of the mountainside. At the entrance to this vault was placed a door said to have been made of iron. Legend tells us that Apaches wiped out the little mining camp in 1769 and concealed the vault door by piling rocks and earth over it. Many searches for the lost Mine With the Iron Door have failed.

Pima County—In 1751, when word was received at Tumacacori Mission that the Indians were in revolt against their Spanish masters, hurried preparations were made to conceal the entrances to the mission's several mines, and to transport the accumulated treasure to a place of safekeeping. All through the night faithful Indians carried bars of gold and silver and stacked them on a **carreta** drawn up before the mission patio. Then followed the church fixtures and all the ornaments that could be carried away. When all was ready, a padre brought out a copper box containing detailed locations to the gold and silver mines, and the **carreta** bumped off across the valley toward the distant mountains to the northwest.

On the second day of the journey, the **carreta** was bouncing through a little canyon in the foothills of the Tascosa Mountains when it was overtaken by a padre afoot, leading a small band of Indians and eight heavily-loaded pack mules. They were from the Mission Altar in Sonora, and the mules were carrying the treasures from that mission's rich mines, being taken north because of an uprising in their region. As the padres discussed their plight, a runner appeared with word that an Apache war party was in the area. They hurriedly dragged their combined treasure into a nearby abandoned mine tunnel. Its entrance was concealed, the **carreta** was abandoned, and the Indian neophytes were told to shift for themselves. Mounting mules, the padres rode off, never to be heard of again.

In the early 1880's a Mexican cowboy, rounding up stray cattle in the Tascosa foothills, came upon the remains of an ancient **carreta** in a small canyon. Nearby he picked up a few rocks from what appeared to be an old mine dump. They revealed traces of silver and he showed them to his boss, who had no interest in the matter and the incident was soon forgotten.

A few years later a party of soldiers chased a band of Apaches into a small canyon in the Tascosas, lost them, and in making their way out, noted the remains of an old **carreta**. They knew nothing of its significance, and since that time the canyon has been known as Carreta Canyon. All searches for the old carreta have failed, and it is presumed to have been washed away by a flash flood, or perhaps covered with debris falling from the canyon wall.

Pima County—A dirt road runs west from Cortaro (Interstate 10) to the virtually extinct town of Silver Bell. The road approximates the old stage route. A stage was once held up on this road by three men in a small mountain pass. Taking the strongbox containing $50,000 in silver dollars, they let the stage proceed. Less than two hours later a posse overtook the three robbers near the scene of the holdup. Two of the bandits were killed outright and the third soon died of his wounds. The empty strongbox was found, but no trace of the treasure could be located. It was said that a drunken woman later stumbled onto the cache, removed $9,000, buried the remainder, but was never able later to find it.

Pima County—After the Civil War an unnamed easterner set out for the west to regain his health. He eventually landed in Tucson and formed a partnership with another man. They outfitted themselves and set out for the little mining camp of Quijotoa at the northern end of the Quijotoa Mountains.

After making a rich strike, the two partners sold their claim and dissolved their partnership, and each set out on his separate way. The easterner, having regained his health, was crossing the desert between Gunsight and Clarkston when he was attracted by a large number of rocks scattered across the floor of a small basin. His examination disclosed that they were rich in silver. A search of the area revealed no ledge, and he figured they were too scattered to have been dropped by a prospector. He broke some of the rocks up, packed them on his mules and proceeded to Yuma. From here the rocks were shipped down the Colorado River to the Gulf of California and from there to the east coast and milled.

A wealthy man from his two finds, the easterner never returned to the west. So far as it is known, the basin with the silver-loaded rocks has never been found again.

Pima County—The Sopori mine was known all over Arizona for its richness in both gold and silver. Supposedly it was discovered by Spaniards following in the wake of Coronado, worked by the Jesuit padres for a time, and either fell into the hands of the owners of the Sopori Ranch, or was "lost" and later found. Popularly, its location is placed on the 21,000-acre Sopori Ranch in southern Pima County, but early Spanish and American maps located it in the northern end of the Cerro Colorado Mountains, where the ruins of an adobe smelter and a crude arrastre were once found. On a hill projecting into Altar Valley, east of the Baboquivari Mountains, were found the ruins of an old wall believed to have been an old mission, or visita, the name of which has been lost for centuries. It is thought that the people who

ARIZONA

lived at this mission once supervised Indians working the Sopori Mine.

The Sopori Ranch was located along the Altar Road, a well-traveled highway from Sonora to San Xavier del Bac Mission. Astride the most important road in southern Arizona, the location of the ranch was strategic in those days. It was an area noted for Apache raids, and the ranch was frequently attacked and many of its people killed from time to time. Just before one of these raids occurred, a large amount of silver and gold from the mine is said to have been buried in one corner of an old adobe house that stood on the ranch. This treasure, according to most accounts, has never been found.

Tradition has it also that the mine was so poorly operated that the rich vein was lost Interest then waned in the mine and it was eventually closed and its site completely lost.

Some extensive research should turn up the location of the old ranch ruins, if any exist, but locating the Lost Sopori Mine will be another matter.

Pima County—The Black Princess is a natural rock formation on the crest of the Cerro Colorado Mountains. The Indians have long held it in a combination of fear and reverence. Resembling the outstretched body of a woman, there are many Opata and Papago legends pertaining to it. This natural figure should not be confused with the Sleeping Beauty formation which is visible from US 70 just south of Globe.

About the time the troops were withdrawn from Arizona at the start of the Civil War, two Mayo Indian brothers came to the Arivaca country from southern Sonora. Their names were Juan and Fermin Morales. Juan was a blonde and his people knew him as "El Guero Mayo."

Juan and Fermin made a living by panning the placers along Arivaca Creek, and in the surrounding mountains. As time went by, Juan, the blonde Mayo, spent more and more time making long excursions into the mountains, while Fermin stayed behind to tend the camp. One day Juan returned from the mountains with his six burros loaded down with rich gold quartz. The brothers crushed the ore in an **arrastre** which they built along Arivaca Creek a few miles north of the present town of Arivaca.

Each week for many months at a time, Juan made the trip into the mountains in the direction of the Black Princess and each time he returned with his six mules loaded with all the gold ore they could carry. Years went by and the endless stream of ore poured into the **arrastre** along Arivaca Creek. The brothers grew rich and they began to spend more leisure time in Arivaca, where they were free with their gold. They engaged in ranching, establishing themselves below the Black Princess where they could presumably keep an eye on their mine.

There are many who believe that the Morales brothers were looking for a particular mine when they came north to Arizona, and that they found it. There are those, too, who believe that the brothers found the Lost Sopori Mine. The Sopori, according to some stories, could have produced

55

the kind of wealth Juan and Fermin Morales accumulated. Juan Morales died in Sonora while on a visit there. Fermin lived until the 1900's and still resided in Arivaca when he died. So far as it is known they never told a single soul the secret location of their mine, and supposedly it is still there waiting to be found.

Pima County—John Clark came to Arizona from Missouri in the early 1850's to prospect for gold and silver. He was attracted to the Cerro Colorado Mountains by the reports of rich ores to be found there. He located a silver claim and eagerly started to work. It was an area where Indian raids were frequent and troops had to provide protection for the miners. Clark's mine was isolated and he had a transportation problem until he made arrangements to ship his ore out with the caravans from the famed Heintzelman Mine. One shipment of 40 tons is said to have netted Clark $80,000 at the then current price of $1 per ounce.

In 1861 the soldiers stationed in Arizona were withdrawn because of the Civil War. This left the miners at the mercy of raiding Apache hordes. Terror gripped the region as one massacre followed another. Most of the settlers fled to the safety of Tucson or left the country entirely. Just as the troops left the area, Clark had another 40 tons of ore mined and stored in a small rock structure near the entrance to his shaft. Aware that he could not move the ore without a military escort, he threw it back into the mine, closed the shaft and concealed its presence.

John Clark then went east to wait until the Indian troubles subsided. While there he died. He talked many times of his rich mine, and he is known to have had considerable wealth. He said that nobody would ever find the mine because he had cleverly covered all traces of it. It is believed that the few men who ever saw Clark's mine were killed in Apache raids or themselves had left the country and never returned.

In 1886 the Apache menace was all but over. It might seem that in this span of time someone would have remembered the location of Clark's mine. It is claimed that this is not the case, and that the mine is still there.

Pima County—A few days after Christmas Day, 1905, a strange marriage took place in a hospital in Quincy, Illinois. The bridegroom was De Estine Shepherd, a man who was gravely ill and aware that he had but a few days to live. The bride was a boardinghouse keeper where Shepherd had lived a short time. The marriage had been conveniently arranged so that he could pass on to her the secret of a mine in Arizona, and in order that she could become heir to a cache of gold ore he said was worth $5,000,000.

De Estine Shepherd had prospected around Arivaca for several years and had struck it rich in the mountains to the southwest. After working the mine for 20 years or so, old age was approaching and he went east to Quincy to locate a brother with whom he had lost contact. The search proved

56

ARIZONA

futile. His health failed rapidly and he was finally informed by his doctor that he had but a short time to live. Having no other relatives, he decided to make it possible for his landlady to become heir to the fortune stored in his mine in Arizona.

The landlady accepted the offer and went through with the ceremony. Shepherd then informed her that she would find a detailed map to the mine in a trunk he had left with a friend in Tucson, Arizona. Shepherd died a few days after the marriage, and it was not long before the widow and her attorney went to Tucson to locate the trunk. The party entrusted with the trunk had moved to Mexico, but they learned that the trunk, for some unexplained reason, had been shipped to Omaha, Nebraska.

With the meager information the widow possessed, she hired a guide and spent several fruitless months searching the area southwest of Arivaca. She finally gave up in despair and returned to Quincy where she shortly remarried. Now the newlyweds started a search in Omaha for the trunk, soon learning that it had been sold at an unclaimed freight sale. Eventually they located the purchaser, who claimed that he had destroyed the map and other papers in the trunk, not realizing their importane. Supposedly, De Estine Shepherd's rich mine and $5,000,000 worth of stored ore is still missing.

Pima County—In the late years of the 17th century, an Irish adventurer named Patrick O'Donahue came to Mexico with the Spanish forces as a soldier of fortune. Through his daring deeds and devoted loyalty to the Spanish Crown, he won considerable recognition. One of the rewards he received from the King of Spain was a grant of 60,000 acres in what is now the southwestern corner of Pima County.

Patrick O'Donahue adopted a Spanish version of his name and became Pedriac Odonoju. With a small band of followers, he moved to his barren desert estate and began the construction of a hacienda. To supply the spiritual needs of his people, he built a small mission and brought in a few priests. The mission was given the name of The Four Evangelists.

Under Don Pedriac's industrious guidance, the mission and the hacienda flourished. It was noted for the hospitality extended Spanish and Indians alike. Friendly Papagos provided abundant labor. Among the gifts they brought to Don Pedriac were nuggets of gold. When they saw how much the gold pleased their benefactor, they brought in more and more. Eventually, the wealth of the hacienda swelled to vast proportions.

But all this was too good to last. On night Apaches swept down on the hacienda and in a burst of savage fury, killed every single inhabitant. All the buildings were burned to the ground, and before the passing of many years every trace of the hacienda was obliterated by the elements.

The site of the hacienda is generally placed in the vicinity of what is known today at Papago .Well, almost on the Mexican border west of Organ Pipe Cactus National Monument. There is a possibility that the hacienda buildings may have stood in Mexico. It has always been assumed that Don Pedriac's wealth would have been buried at the hacienda.

Pima County—In 1884, four masked men held up a Southern Pacific passenger train as it stopped for water at the little tank town of Pantano southeast of Tucson. They made away with $62,000 in gold coins consigned to meet Tucson payrolls and to pay the troops stationed at Fort Lowell. Sheriff Robert Leatherwood and a posse picked up the trail almost immediately, and traced the outlaws to a "hole in the ground" now known as Colossal Cave, on the slope of Wrong Mountain in the Rincon Range about 27 miles southeast of Tucson.

After days of waiting for the bandits to emerge from the cave, a cowboy rode in with the news that four men were whooping it up in the saloons of Willcox, spending gold coins and laughing about how they had outwitted the posse by sneaking out of the cave through a second and distant entrance. Leatherwood rode to Willcox, recruited a local posse, and located the four strangers. In a shootout that followed, three of the outlaws were killed and the fourth, Phil Carver, newest member of the gang, was captured. Before leaving for prison to serve a 28-year term, the prisoner revealed that most of the contents of the sacks of gold had been buried in the cave by the three dead men while he had stood guard at the entrance. A three-day search of the cave revealed no treasure, and it was not until years later that the second entrance to the cave was discovered.

When Carver was released from prison, a Wells Fargo agent was on hand to trail him. He went immediately to Tucson where he soon gave the agent the slip. In examining the cave several days later, empty money sacks were found deep in the cavern, but because of the dry nature of the cave, it could not be determined if they had been opened and discarded recently or many years ago. The question remains unsolved—does Colossal Cave, now a county park with guides to conduct tours through it, still hold a major portion of the Pantano train robbery treasure?

Pima County—The Southern Pacific tank town of Pantano, now a ghost, is located just off Interstate 10 about 21 miles southeast of Tucson. Two and one-half miles west of Pantano, and directly under the Southern Pacific right-of-way, is the site of the old Butterfield Overland Mail station of La Cienega, known also as Cienega. The original site of the station was located a short distance from here at a point now lost. It is this site that this story is concerned with.

In 1872 the original Cienega station was operated by a small band of outlaws known locally as the "Benders," presumably from the many drunken sprees held there. Murders, robberies and holdups occurred here regularly, and with practically no interference from authorities. On a small hill back of the station, the outlaws had a private cemetery for their victims, and for many years a single shaft marked the graves of 18 unknown dead.

ARIZONA

Most of the crimes committed in the area were the work of the Benders disguised at Apaches. Their most important haul was $75,000 secured in the ambush of an army patrol near the station. The money is said to have been buried at a spot near the station, and before it could be taken out of the country, a band of real Apaches swarmed down on the station and murdered the Benders to a man.

In 1897 four strange men spent some time at the site of the old Cienega station and turned away any curious onlookers who came near. A few days later they appeared in Tucson with some sacks which they said contained ore samples. When they rode out of Tucson it was noted that the sacks went with them. Teamsters working in the area reported the finding of several holes, both inside and outside the half-ruined adobe structure. Sometime later ranchers probing the place uncovered 300 American dollars in the fireplace of the station. This find stirred many other and more extensive searches, but nothing is known to have been found. No one knows for certain whether or not the four mysterious strangers found and hauled away the treasure of the Benders. If the original site of the station can be located, it may still bear investigation.

Pima County—When southern Arizona still belonged to Mexico, and many years before Americans came to the region to search for mineral wealth, the Papago Indians are said to have worked the arroyos around the great copper deposits at Ajo for gold which they took to Caborca, in Sonora, and used for trading purposes. While the Indians generally did not mine gold except under compulsion, it is believed that they were not above picking up surface nuggets to use in bartering.

When the Mexicans learned of this gold, they sent an expedition northward, dispossessed the Papagos and assumed possession of the placers. Being a peace-loving people, the Papago simply walked away and let the Mexicans take over.

After working the placers for several months and accumulating a considerable hoard of gold, which was stored in a large earthen pot known as an **olla**, a band of Apaches invaded the area and attacked. The Mexicans defended themselves as best they could, but they were outnumbered. Those who were not killed fled to Mexico, leaving behind the **olla** of gold buried in the ground near the camp which the Apaches destroyed.

Unknown to either the Mexicans or the Apaches, the displaced Papagos watched the battle from concealment in the nearby hills. The Apaches were their traditional enemies, but the Papagos had no weapons with which to attack. Their old medicine man came to the front and revealed that he had a weapon that would destroy the hated Apaches. From a buckskin bag worn around his neck, he produced a handful of white powder and tossed it into the air. This was supposed to create a sandstorm that would destroy everything in its path, and according to Papago legend, this is exactly what happened. The Apaches fled in panic and the Papagos recovered their placers.

The Papagos knew nothing of the buried olla of gold, which is supposedly still buried where the Mexicans placed it. It is said that the Papagos still gather at Moivavi, the Indian name for Ajo, each year to celebrate their great victory over the Apaches.

Pima County—In the early 1870's, a troop of soldiers from Fort Tucson were engaged in chasing a band of Apaches toward the Mexican border. If the Indians succeeded in crossing over into Mexico, they could not be brought back to their reservation, so in spite of the terrifc heat the soldiers pressed hard to overtake them.

Somewhere in the Baboquivari Mountains the troops were brought to a halt in a small canyon where a pool of cool water had collected at the foot of a rocky ledge. A second pool was found near the first and the men split into two groups so that they could all gather around the welcome water. As one of the soldiers kneeled to fill his canteen, he noticed that the bottom of the pool was covered with bright shining pebbles. H scooped up a handful and showed them to his companions. Someone recognized the pebbles as gold nuggets and there was a wild scramble to fill their pockets. More nuggets were found along the ledge and the men, forgetting their fatigue, rushed madly to gather as many as they could before ordered to resume the chase.

When the officer in charge gave the command to mount, several of the men expressed their desire to abandon the chase and collect the gold. But the order stood and their request was denied. As the soldiers rode away, the men tried to locate landmarks in their minds so that they could return at a later date. But in a country where all the landscape looks remarkably alike, it takes an extremely experienced man to retrace his steps weeks or months later.

Eventually the fleeing Indians were headed off, captured and returned to Tucson. The soldiers did not forget the gold. Some asked to be discharged, but were denied. Two of the more determined, deserted, stole mounts and rode away to the south. They eventually found the ledge, but the water in the pools they depended upon had dried up. Nevertheless, they gathered all the gold they could carry, and loaded their horses so heavily that they were forced to walk and lead the animals. Before long the extreme heat began to take its toll and they had to lighten their animals' burdens. Time and time again they discarded some of the gold. One of the horses fell and could not rise. Before long the second horse dropped of thirst and exhaustion.

When a search party found the deserters, one was dead and the other was in a dying condition. Before death claimed him he managed to gasp out an account of their experiences. It is said that several of the men who had seen the gold in the two "tanks" in the Baboquivari Mountains made searches after they were discharged from the army. If any ever found it the news was kept a secret.

Pima County—The legendary treasure of Montezuma is reportedly buried in at least a dozen different places ranging from Utah to Mexico, and from California to Texas. To make matters more confusing, there were two Montezumas—one was the legendary Indian god of New Mexico, and the other was the Aztec ruler of Mexico who was overthrown by Cortez.

When word was brought to the great Montezuma at his capital in what is now Mexico City that strange men had arrived in boats at Vera Cruz, he did not know that they were Spaniards bent on their national past-time of treasure hunting. Montezuma believed that they might be representatives of the Aztec's traditional sun god Quetzalcoatl, whom it was thought would return to them someday. If such was the case, the strange men must be royally welcomed. If, on the other hand, they were not, the vast treasures of the Aztec empire might be in danger. Montzuma was in a quandry.

In the days before the arrival of the Spaniards in Vera Cruz, Montezuma had made war each year upon the Tlaxcaltecans. In one of these raids he captured the enemy's famous general, Tlahuicole, and had him taken to Mexico City to be offered up as a sacrifice. But instead of suffering this fate, Tlahuicole became a great favorite of Montezuma, who admired his strength and courage.

On the arrival of the Spaniards in Mexico, Montezuma sent them many rich presents. Their reception of these gifts and the demand for more convinced the Aztec emperor that they were not descendants of the sun god, but only avaricious men in search of gold. Summoning Tlahuicole, Montezuma instructed him to take one-half of the empire's enormous wealth far to the north and hide it so well that no enemy could ever find it. According to this version of the story, the vast treasure was taken into Arizona and hidden in a cave in the mountains near Ajo, where it remains to this day.

Other sites in Arizona claimed to be the traditional burial place of the Montezuma fortune are the ruins of Casa Grande National Monument, nine miles west of Florence, Pinal County, and Montezuma Well, in Montezuma Castle National Monument. There is no question but that Montezuma possessed an enormous hoard of gold and silver. The Spaniards succeeded in grabbing tons of it, and other great amounts were dumped into the lake surrounding the original Aztec capital. It appears to be logical that a part of the vast treasure was removed from Mexico City when the true intentions of the Spaniards were made clear. In Mexico, the tradition persists that this treasure was secreted on Tiburon Island in the Gulf of California.

Pima County—Samuel P. Heintzelman, a man well known in Arizona mining history, once noted a piece of gray silver ore in Warner's Store in Tucson. Inquiry revealed that a Mexican had brought the ore in and traded it, and Heintzelman set out to find him. When finally located, the Mexican refused to reveal where he had secured the ore. Heintzelman offered him $500 for the secret, but when the Mexican demanded cash on the line, Heintzelman refused. Finally it was agreed that the $500 would be held by

Solomon Warner and paid to the Mexican when definite proof of the ore in quantity was produced.

Heintzelman and the Mexican traveled south and made camp at the foot of a small red mountain known as Cerro Chiquito. On the following morning the Mexican showed Heintzelman where the ore was located on the slope of the mountain. It was almost pure silver. Filling their saddlebags, the men returned to Tucson where the Mexican demanded his $500. Heintzelman handed him a 50-cent piece and said, "Here, this is enough for a Mexican!"

Heintzelman lost no time in developing the mine, taking out $100,000 in the first year of operation. The property was then sold to the Sonora Exploring and Mining Co., of which Charles D. Poston, a prominent Arizona pioneer, was one of the organizers. John Poston, brother of Charles, was placed in charge of the rich producer. Mexicans said the mine was cursed because it had been stolen from one of their people. When 15 Mexican and Indian workers were entombed in the depths of the mine by a cave-in, the Mexicans were more certain than ever that the mine was evil. Heintzelman had named the mine the Cerro Colorado after a nearby reddish mountain, but to the Mexicans it was known as the Cursed Cerro Colorado.

With the beginning of the Civil War, the troops which provided protection for the mine were withdrawn and the Apaches immediately began to make good their threats to drive all white men from their lands. And there was other trouble in store for Cerro Colorado. With the mine guards reduced in number, Mexicans began stealing the rich ore right and left. Matters were brought to a head when John Poston caught his Mexican mine foreman heading south with a heavy load of stolen silver. Poston killed him in cold blood. This act brought a halt to all work in the mine, and the enraged miners carried away everything they could load on mules.

Learning of the helpless condition of the mine from fleeing miners, a band of outlaws swooped down on the Cerro Colorado, killed John Poston and two other men, and all but tore the mine apart searching for the silver supposed to be stored there. But the silver had already been stolen by the revolting miners. The story persists that $70,000 of this stolen bullion was buried on the slope of Cerro Colorado facing the mine on Cerro Chiquito. Supposedly this bullion has never been recovered.

Pima County—According to an old Indian legend, a party of Spanish priests and friendly Indians were traveling through the Rincon Mountains southeast of Tucson in search of a suitable country in which to establish a rancheria. They found no place to their satisfaction, but they did find gold and accumulated a great quantity of it which they packed on their horses and headed back to Sonora.

Weaving their way through the lower stretches of the Rincons, they were suddenly attacked by a band of Apaches, who were more interested in securing their horses than the gold. The Sonorans successfully fought off the attack with only a small loss of life. But the Apaches captured their

ARIZONA

horses and fled with the still-loaded animals. In a nearby mountainside cave, the gold was concealed and the Apaches rode off. It is said that this treasure has never been recovered.

Most of the Rincon Range is within the boundaries of Saguaro National Monument.

Pima County—Old Indian legends tell of a treasure vault built into the walls of Canada del Oro (Canyon of Gold) where the gold taken from the Escalante Mine (Mine With the Iron Door) was stored in anticipation that the Jesuits might have to flee the country on short notice. This occasion arose in 1769 while the miners were celebrating San Juan's Day. A party of Apaches swept out of the hills and annihilated the Indians. The padres managed to escape to Sonora and never returned to recover the treasure in the secret vault.

On detailed maps of Arizona will be found a Canada del Oro on the western slopes of the Santa Catalina Mountains between Tucson and Oracle. It is skirted on the west by US 80-89.

Pima County—Almost all southwestern Indians are said to have some sort of tribal law against revealing the location of gold and silver ores and buried treasures to white men. The reason was one of simple preservation for the Indians. They knew the white man's maniacal greed for gold and the results of their finding it on Indian lands.

An old Papago frequently came into the old Spanish settlement in Arivaca, located a few miles up Arivaca Creek from the present town of that name. In exchange for gold nuggets he secured supplies and provisions. Any Indian or Mexican of the time who wanted to work could, with a little exertion, gather up an ounce or more of gold a day along Arivaca Creek, so the old Papago's handful of gold nuggets never excited anyone very much. But as the years went by and the surface gold along Arivaca Creek gave out, the old Papago still brought in his regular supply of gold nuggets. People began to take notice. It was guessed by some that he might have a secret mine someplace in the Baboquivari Mountains where he lived most of the time in a crude hut.

There were stories that the Spanish had once worked a rich old mine in the Baboquivari Mountains, and some thought the old Papago might have stumbled upon it. No amount of persuasion would induce him to give out a bit of information. He made his purchases and plodded back to his mountain retreat, cunningly avoiding any followers. One day he moved his few belongings to a new home along Arivaca Creek, and this aroused talk that his secret source of gold was exhausted. He soon disproved this by continuing to make his frequent exchange of gold for supplies.

It was quite a surprise one day, then, when he voluntarily told the merchant where he did his trading the secret of his gold. This was the story he told.

TREASURE GUIDE

One evening when he was out hunting on the slopes of the Baboquivari Mountains he sat down to rest. His attention was drawn to a large number of bats emerging from a distant hole in the ground. Aware that bats live in caves, he decided to investigate the following day. He located the cave from which he had seen the bats emerge, poked his way through a narrow tunnel, and found that ore had been taken from its walls. There was a draft in the tunnel so he looked about and found a second opening farther down the mountain side. This opened into a large cavern, the entrance of which was almost concealed with brush and debris. Clearing some of this away, he discovered it to be a mine shaft, the floor of which was littered with rotted timbers, rusted tools and pieces of equipment which he recognized as being of Spanish origin. Stacked along one of the walls was a neat row of rotted buckskin bags filled with gold nuggets. He guessed that these had been gathered in another part of the mountain and brought here for storage. In a corner was a pile of gold bars which he assumed had been smelted nearby.

There was no question but what the old Papago had found an old Spanish mine, and that it contained riches enough for a rajah. There were legends of several located in the area. With the revelation of all these details, the merchant listened eagerly, expecting to inherit the secret. But all the aged Indian would say was that it was located in the Baboquivari Mountains. He had taken out enough gold to last him a life-time, after which he had closed both entrances so that flights of bats could never again reveal its location. The old Papago had not betrayed his people by telling a white man exactly where gold could be found.

Pinal County—During the Indian troubles in Arizona, the Army maintained a military camp near Picket Post Mountain atop of which was a heliograph station. Camp Picket Post eventually became the town on Picket Post, and later became known as Pinal, now a ghost town. Stationed at the post was an army detail constructing a military road which today roughly parallels State 77 between Globe and Winkelman.

While returning to camp from work one day in 1872, a soldier named Sullivan discovered a rich outcropping of silver. He knew nothing of metals but kept the piece of rich ore. Soon after receiving his discharge he began a fruitless attempt to interest settlers in the Florence area in grubstaking him to locate and mine a ledge he had found. No one listened to him for three years. Finally a rancher named Charles G. Mason gave him a few clothes for a description of the site. Sullivan was never heard of again.

Mason organized a party of three others, and following Sullivan's directions located the ledge, a definite instance of a "lost" mine being found. In March, 1875, they filed on the Silver King Mine which became one of the richest silver mines in the world.

During the height of the excitement caused by the finding of the Silver King, two soldiers of French-Canadian descent were discharged at Fort McDowell and joined in the search for more of the silver that had caused such

64

a sensation. Plodding through the Superstitions one day, they flushed a deer. One of the men raised his rifle and fired. The deer bounded away unharmed as the bullet plowed into a reddish rock ledge, dislodging several pieces. The soldiers pocketed a few pieces of the ore and continued on their way. They, too, knew little of precious ores.

Having worked their way across country to the Silver King Mine, and being broke and disgusted with prospecting, they asked for and were given jobs. In time they showed the reddish ore to the mine foreman, Jack Frazier. An expert mining man, Frazier recognized the ore to be gold in an almost native state. He estimated its value to be enormous.

Frazier offered to grubstake the two ex-soldiers if they would retrace their steps and locate the ledge. They agreed, and for a fifty percent interest, the foreman established a $500 credit for them at the Silver King commissary store. They drew out $265 worth of provisions and set out. It is a matter of record that a $265 credit still showed on the commissary's books when the Silver King Mine closed. The two men never returned.

Somebody later recalled that when the two ex-soldiers rode away from the camp, they were followed by a lone rider named Smith, a camp gambler. Smith later turned up in Alaska, a wealthy man. The implication was clear— Smith had murdered the two men when they located the ledge, took out a quantity of the rich ore, and then fearing that he would be caught and charged with the killings, fled the country. The bodies of the two men were later found on the southern slopes of the Superstitions, and there was speculation that they had stumbled upon Jacob Walz's Lost Dutchman Mine. Frazier did not believe so. He hired other men to search for the reddish ore, and claimed to know approximately where it was located, but so far as it is known, the Lost Ledge of the Two Soldiers has never been found.

Pinal County—Of all the lost mine legends of the west, that of the Lost Dutchman is the most widely told, the most written about, the most searched for, and the most confusing in its many variations. Hundreds of theories have been presented by serious students of the legend, and an untold number of men have lost their lives in searching for the Dutchman's source of gold in the Superstition Mountains.

The saga of the Lost Dutchman begins in Mexico, when a young lad named Manuel Peralta, denied the hand of the girl he loved, fled northward from the wrath of his sweetheart's irate father. In the Superstition Mountains he found rich gold ore, and armed with a supply of this he returned to Mexico. Led by his father, the whole Peralta clan prepared to journey north to work the rich mine the young man had found. By the time they started they were 400 strong. They had no difficulty in locating the source of the gold. When they had taken out all the ore their mules could carry, they headed back for Mexico.

Winding their way down the rugged canyons, they were hardly out of sight of the mine when overwhelming numbers of Apaches struck with deadly fury. All except two young boys, who managed to hide in the bushes and later make their escape, were annihilated. Then the Indians hid all the gold carried by the mules and obliterated all traces of the mine so that it could never be found again. The two young boys, both Peraltas, survived their ordeal and finally made their way back to Mexico. When they grew up they took a third party into their confidence and returned to the Superstitions. After considerable searching they located the old Peralta mine through secret marks that had been left by the original party. They had hardly begun to take out the ore when the Dutchman appeared.

The Dutchman was a white-bearded old prospector named Jacob Walz. He was picking his way through the Superstitions one day early in the 1870's, and to escape a band of Apaches, he fled into a section of the mountains he had never before visited. He stumbled straight into the camp of the three Peralta miners. They were glad to have his company and accepted him as a friend. Walz observed the rich ore they were taking out, and that it seemed to exist in limitless quantities. Watching his chance, he turned on the three miners and killed them. From that time on until his death in 1891, the fabulous mine that became the Lost Dutchman was his alone.

When the news of the fabulous find became common knowledge through Walz's open boasting in Phoenix, prospectors tried to trail him into the mountains, but he either outwitted them or killed them from ambush. For years Walz played this game of hide and seek with his followers, seeming content to bring out only enough ore at a time to finance a prolonged drinking spree.

In 1877 the years were catching up with Walz and he decided to retire. He bought or rented a small plat of ground and an adobe hut along the Salt River on the outskirts of Phoenix and settled down to occasional farming, but mostly hitting the bottle. Now and then he disappeared, and always returned with a supply of ore. He made friends with Julia Thomas, a Negress, and she cared for him when he was ill. The only other close friend he was known to have had was a German baker named Reinhart Petrash.

After the Dutchman's death in 1891, Julia Thomas said she possessed a map showing the location of the mine, which she claimed Walz had given her. According to the Negress, Walz had told her that the mine consisted of an 18-inch vein of rose quartz heavily impregnated with gold nuggets. A second vein of hematite quartz was one-third pure gold. After working both veins for years, according to Walz, he was not even near their depletion. He estimated that there was at least $100,000,000 to be taken out. According to the Dutchman's directions, there was a cave in a secluded spot of the Superstitions in which he hid when eluding followers. About a mile from the cave there was a rock resembling a face looking to the east. To the south was Weaver's Needle (long a popular landmark associated with the Lost Dutchman Mine). Follow the right of two canyons beyond the Needle, he directed, but not too far. The mine faced west and at certain times of the year, the setting sun shone through a pass between two high ridges and fell directly on the mine's covered entrance.

Julia Thomas and Reinhart Petrash searched unsuccessfully for the Dutchman's mine for almost three years. Throughout the succeeding years, thousands of prospectors, professional and amateur, have sought the Lost Dutchman Mine. Many have never returned from the Superstitions.

This, briefly, is the story of the Lost Dutchman Mine. There are many, many theories, variations, contradictions and clues—and almost yearly reports that the famed mine has been found. Where does fiction end and fact begin? There is no substantiation of the Peralta part of the story, but beyond a questionable doubt there was a white-bearded Dutchman named Jacob Walz, and he did show up in Phoenix at intervals with a sack of rich gold ore and nuggets. If he didn't secure it from the old Peralta mine, assuming that there was one, then where did it come from? Some skeptics have an answer.

Jacob Walz, they point out, had been attracted to Arizona by the sensational news of the discovery of the Vulture Mine by Henry Wickenburg. For a brief time he was employed at the Vulture, but was fired for "high-grading"—stealing ore from the mine. He concealed this ore, eventually packed it into the Superstitions where he cached it, and drew upon it as his drinking habits required.

In spite of fantastic claims, the Superstitions are no more dangerous than any other desert mountains. The many stories of mysterious killings in the Superstitions are highly exaggerated. There have been many deaths there, to be sure, but mostly they have been the result of a lack of knowledge of the mountains. A properly prepared party having common sense understanding of desert heat and mountain cold, and the conservation of one's strength, need not have any fear of the Superstitions.

Pinal County—In 1882 a Dr. Thorne (his first name may have been Abraham, the point is not clear) supposedly a medical man with some experience in the army at old Camp McDowell, told a story of being captured by Apache Indians and forced to live with them for some four years. During his captivity Thorne successfully performed surgery upon the broken kneecap of an Indian boy. This so impressed the Indians that they thereafter treated the doctor with a great deal of respect, but still kept him in capivity. The young man assigned to him as a servant, according to Thorne's story, was actually a guard to see that he did not escape. One day as the two were hunting together, they boy picked up a gold nugget in the bed of a wash believed to have been in the Superstition Mountains southeast of Phoenix. Thorne pretended to be disinterested in the gold, but carefully noted that some $5,000 could probably have been picked up on the surface of the wash.

It was a year later that Thorne managed to escape while the Apaches were celebrating the making of a treaty with the Navajos as they camped in the Mogollon Mountains. Later he made several efforts to locate the gold, leading expeditions into the Superstitions. Nothing came from these searches and Dr. Thorne slowly passed from history. The very reputable Arizona historian, James H. McClintock, says that Dr. Thorne was eventually exposed and denounced as an imposter. But there are people who still believe that Dr. Thorne's Lost Mine really exists.

Pinal County—A prospector known only as Wagoner frequently rode the Pinal-Mesa stage from Pinal to the western edge of the Superstitions, where he would take off afoot in the direction of Apache Gap. On his return trip he always caught the stage in the same lonely spot. Usually the two sacks in which he carried provisions were empty on the homeward trip. When he was broke, which was most of the time, the stage driver obligingly carried him without pay.

One day Wagoner changed his stage boarding and unboarding place to a spot near Whitlow's ranch, and the two provision sacks were replaced with expensive looking leather suitcases. When he returned from the mountains, the driver noted, the suitcases appeared to be full and heavy. About a week would pass between the time Wagoner left the stage and made his return. The stage driver guessed that Wagoner had found something in the mountains, but it was not the custom of the day to ask questions.

Sometimes a curious party would try to trail Wagoner, but the lone prospector was apparently too wise to be followed. There were rumors that he was selling quantities of free gold. He paid the stagedriver for the free trips he had been given and he always appeared to have plenty of money.

One day Wagoner appeared at his usual boarding place, and the driver noted that he appeared to be ill and weak. In fact, Wagoner asked the driver to load the suitcases for him, something that he had never done before. Remarking about their great weight, Wagoner replied that it was his last trip into the mountains and that it would be all right if he wished to examine the contents. Opening one of the bags, the driver found it full of extremely rich gold ore.

"You may as well have the mine," Wagoner said. "You carried me free when nobody else would stake me." And then he gave the driver instructions for finding the outcropping of rose quartz from which the gold had been taken. It was covered with brush and lay hidden within a circle of new trees which had been planted as a landmark. Wagoner said he had enough gold to last a lifetime and he was going to return east and retire.

The stagedriver never located the ledge, nor did the man who turned up 20 years later with a map purportedly drawn by Wagoner as he lay on his deathbed in a hospital. This map supposedly described the ledge as being in La Barge Canyon. La Barge, after whom the canyon and the creek were named, was a French prospector whose camp was at a spring at the base of Weaver's Needle. He had been a one-time companion of Jacob Walz, and after Walz's death, he spent the remainder of his life searching for the Dutchman's Lost Mine. It has often been surmised that the Dutchman's mine and Wagoner's were the same.

Pinal County—One day in 1937, Bill Jenkins, his wife and their two daughters picnicked as they frequently did on his day off from his job in Phoenix. They selected a site along the slopes of the Superstition Mountains, and while Bill climbed a slope to get a better view of Weaver's Needle, his family remained at the picnic site. Mrs. Jenkins collected specimens of pretty rocks, and when Bill arrived back at their car, he noted that one of the rocks was very heavy and that there were many more of the same kind in the area.

It was many months later that someone in Phoenix told Bill that the rock was rich in gold. Bill had it assayed and it ran $2,000 to the ton. Because of being transferred to another town and World War II coming along, it was ten years before Bill was finally persuaded to lead a search party for the gold. Just as they were prepared to leave, Jenkins dropped dead of a heart attack.

Pinal County—Thomas McLain (sometimes spelled McClean) was a man of high character until he became involved, through his own contrivance or that of others, in a scandal at old Fort Yuma on the Colorado River. He was a graduate of West Point where his heavy head of bushy black hair earned him the nickname of "Buffalo Tom." It is said that he came from a fine eastern family of long-standing military traditions.

In 1849 McLain showed up in the gold camps of California. A few years later he appeared in Arizona as Lt. McLain, acting quartermaster in charge of all army supplies shipped into· Yuma by boat and then trans-shipped to the many inland military posts. The quantity of supplies passing through Fort Yuma was enormous, and the temptation to increase one's meager army pay by diverting some of the supplies must have been great. McLain did not long resist it, but whether or not he concocted the scheme to defraud the government himself, or was the innocent tool of crooked army contractors is not clear. Whatever the circumstances, the story has it that Lt. McLain was courtmartialed from the army and discharged in disgrace.

It seems now that McLain turned his back on white men and did everything in his power to become an Indian. He took up residence with Yumas in the vicinity of the fort. He married the daughter of a chief and was made a full tribal member. From this period on he never used his real name, but was known to white men and red men alike as "Yuma."

Among the Yumas and the Papàgos he was trusted as one of their own, and even the Apaches condescended to trade with him. With his Indian wife serving as a safe passport among the various Indian tribes of southwestern Arizona, he traveled back and forth between Yuma and Tucson, carrying on a profitable trade with the Indians. His pack mules were loaded with firearms, ammunition, calico, beads and such other articles as the Indians cherished. In trade he received coin and gold nuggets.

From his Indian wife, Yuma learned that a local group of Apaches, known as the Aravaipas, possessed a rich mine from which they secured their gold for trading purposes. As they needed the gold they took it out, otherwise keeping the source covered with gravel and brush. The chief **rancheria** of the Aravaipas was located about five miles from old Camp Grant, which was situated at the junction of the San Pedro River and Aravaipa Creek, a few miles southwest of Winkleman in Pinal County. It was near here that Yuma guessed from the information given him by his wife that the rich Aravaipa placer was located.

When Yuma met Es-kim-en-zin, chief of the Aravaipas, he asked to see the mine, presenting the argument that, as a member in good standing, he was only asking for his right to be let in on the secret. The Aravaipa chief was reluctant at first, but finally agreed to take him to the place where the gold was picked up. They traveled in a northwesterly direction from the Aravaipa camp, climbed a long rocky ridge and kept on its crest for about three miles until they came to a range that overlooked San Pedro Valley to the east. Proceeding northward for another six miles, the chief suddenly stopped and announced that this was the place.

From the floor of a depression they were standing in, Yuma scraped away the loose earth with his hands—and there was the ore! While digging out a generous sample with his knife, Yuma carefully observed the surrounding country, making mental notes of any landmarks. They returned to the Aravaipa camp and Yuma remained there several days to avert any suspicion that he was in hurry to leave. When he eventually took leave, he did not return to the mine but rode straight to Tucson.

Up to this point the various accounts of Yuma's Lost Mine are in general agreement. One story now has it that Yuma returned to the Aravaipa placer in 1860 with a Gen. Walker (whether this was Joseph R. Walker or John D. Walker is not clear. Both were prominent in southwestern Arizona about this time). They supposedly filled their saddlebags with the rich ore which they took to Tucson and publicly displayed. There was a lot of excitement, but they told their secret to no one.

In 1861, following the Indian troubles at Camp Grant, Yuma went into the Papago country to roundup the cattle he grazed there. He feared a raid by the Apaches, now that he had betrayed them, and planned to move his herd to safer country. The Papagos took this move to mean that he was joining up with the Apaches, their bitterest enemies. As he slept one night they crept up on McLain and clubbed him to death.

Upon the death of McLain, the secret of the gold mine was now Gen. Walker's. Continued fear of the Apaches kept him away from the gold, and in 1865 he died of tuberculosis. Before his death, however, Walker passed on the secret to a friend, John Sweeny. Sweeney was a heavy boozer, more interested in the bars in Tucson than all the gold in Arizona. For the price of a few whiskeys he sold the secret to one Charles O. Brown, but the directions to the Aravaipa gold were so garbled that Brown was never able to locate it.

When the Aravaipas were virtually wiped out by a white man-inspired band of Papagos and Mexicans at an incident known as the Camp Grant Massacre, it is believed that the secret of the mine was lost even to the Indians.

Pinal County—The town of Red Rock is located on Interstate 10 northwest of Tucson. It takes its name from a prominent red butte in the area of the same name. In a cave between Red Rock Butte and the Silver Bell Mountains to the east is said to be stored an enormous amount of gold and silver gathered by the Papago Indians and turned over to a group of unknown white men who entered the region and lived with them briefly at some unknown early date in history.

One day a band of enemy Indians raided the Papago **rancheria** at Red Rock, killing every white man and burning the village. Believing the stored gold and silver was a curse, the Indians concealed the entrance to the storage cave, and under the penalty of death, forbid any tribesman to reveal its location. The story is strictly legendary, but artifacts found in the Red Rock area are said to be evidence that a strange party of white men visited the region long before the arrival of the Spanish.

Pinal County—Among the many wagon trains making their way overland to the California gold fields in 1849-1850 was one originating in San Antonio, Texas. The party consisted of 14 families, and they were apparently well-to-do, for one of the wagons carried their accumulated fortunes—$50,000—in an iron pot or chest. Each night, for safekeeping, this money was buried within the circle formed by the wagons, and each morning it was dug up and reloaded.

All the way from San Antonio the party had been plagued with Indian troubles. Somewhere along the route, one of the families, fearing to go on, turned back and eventually arrived safely in San Antonio. The others stubbornly proceeded westward. One night they made camp near the natural formation known as Montezuma Head. As was their custom, the wagons were drawn into a circle, campfires were built, the chest of gold was buried, and guards were posted. At daybreak a howling band of Apaches overwhelmed the party and killed every member of the group. Swarming through the wagons, the Indians took what they wanted and then fired the vehicles where they stood.

A short time later an eastbound wagon train arrived in San Antonio and its members reported having passed the site of the massacre. Hearing the news, members of the family that had turned back to San Antonio recognized the massacred train as the one they had been with and revealed the story of the wealth they buried every night. Because of hostile Apaches in the area, no immediate search was made for the wagon train treasure, and in time the incident was all but forgotten. Many years later the remains of a circle of burned wagons was found near Montezuma Head and this recalled the buried treasure. A search was made for the wealth, but it is not known that anything was found

Pinal County—The Mission San Marcelo was founded in 1699 by Father Kino for the Papago Indians. It was located about one mile north of the present town of Sonoita (Sonoyta), Sonora, Mexico, just south of the International Line. It is said that the Indians of San Marcelo Mission worked rich mines, one of which was the fabulously rich Santa Lucia Mine in the Pozo Redondo Mountains. The smelted gold and silver from these mines was normally stored at the mission, but when the Papagos revolted in 1751, this wealth in gold and silver bars was transported north and hidden in a cave in the Tortillita Mountains in southeastern Pinal County, although some accounts place the cave in the Puerto Blanco Mountains in southwestern Pima County.

It is said that this treasure was never recovered because all the padres and Indians knowing its whereabouts were later killed.

Santa Cruz County—One of the first Mexican families to follow Father Eusebio Kino northward into Pimeria Alta was the Valverdes. They settled in the Santa Cruz Valley in the vicinity of Guevavi Mission (now only a mound of rubble, but its site can be located). With their ranch established, the Valverdes took to the surrounding mountains in search of gold which they knew the Indians secured. They found gold at some spot lost to history and developed a rich mine. Employing Indian laborers, the Valverde mine produced enough gold each year that a large pack train was required to carry it out to Mexico. The Valverdes prospered immensely, and to store the wealth of their mine between pack train trips to Mexico, they built a stone vault under the main house of the ranch.

Stinging under the harsh treatment of their Spanish masters, the Indians of Pimeria Alta rose in revolt in 1772, destroyed missions and ranches, and killed all white men who did not flee their wrath. Among the families managing to escape to Mexico were the Valverdes, but they had to leave behind their horses and cattle, and about a year's accumulation of gold.

Wealthy from the gold they had already sent to Mexico, the Valverdes never returned to Arizona. In time, all traces of the ranch were reduced to rubble, and today not even a low mound remains to indicate its site, which is probably overgrown with mesquite and cottonwood trees.

Santa Cruz County—On the border between Arizona and Mexico, just where the International Line makes an angle and turns northwesterly towards the Gulf of California, there is a high mountain in the Pajarito Range which has been known to the Indians for centuries as Cerro Ruido, or Noisy Mountain, because of the strange and unexplained sounds which emanate from it. These sounds have been compared by some to the low rumble of thunder, and others liken them to the sounds of the lowest notes of a pipe organ. Whatever the sound, Cerro Ruido's rocky canyons are filled with legends, and one of these legends is that of a lost mission in its mysterious depths with a vast stored treasure of silver.

There is some evidence that the mission padres, in traveling from their stations in Sonora to those in southern Arizona, frequently took a shorter, but much rougher trail, through the Pajaritos and passed near the base of Cerro Ruido, where stories handed down by generations of local Indians say a mission was located.

The story persists that a large amount of silver bullion was hidden in a cave near the mission to prevent it from falling into the hands of Spanish soldiers sent to collect the **quinta**, royal fifth, claimed by the Spanish Crown. Failure to pay this tribute is believed to have been one of the reasons why the Jesuits were expelled from Spanish possessions in the New World.

Although there is no known record of any mission ever being founded in the Pajaritos, it is entirely possible that one could have been founded, abandoned, and all historical record of it completely lost. The Pajarito Mountains stood squarely across the shortest route between the Arizona chain of missions and the Sonora chain. Father Kino stated in his diary that he crossed these mountains in traveling between the two chains. Cerro Ruido stood one day's journey south of Guevavi, Arizona's southernmost mission. Water was plentiful here and it seems reasonable to assume that this would have been a logical place to establish a mission or **visita**, a stopping place where shelter could be had for the night. It was common practice in both Arizona and California to place missions or **visitas** one day's journey apart.

In 1736, not far south of Cerro Ruido, the Spanish found the famed **planchas de plata** (planks of silver) ore, which became one of the richest silver mines ever discovered in America. Indians worked these mines under supervision of the padres. If the padres were hiding silver from the Spanish, the Pajarito Mountains would have been the logical place to carry this silver.

In 1945 an article appeared in a national magazine reporting the discovery of this mission and its stored silver by two unnamed veterans of World War I. The article carried photos of the mission ruins and described the fabulous cache of silver. This would have appeared to be conclusive evidence that the lost mission and its treasure had been found. Such was not the case, however, Suspicious of the article's authenticity, this writer contacted the editor of the magazine and was informed that the author of the article had heard the story of the lost mission and its treasure from Indians while employed as an engineer laying out the railroad from Nogales to Guadalajara, and had *based* the "factual" article around the legend. The mission had not been found at all and the photos were not genuine.

Nevertheless, the lost mission of Cerro Ruido and its vast treasure of silver may still be a reality. Legends have a hard way of dying and sometimes this is because they are based on facts which have not yet been revealed.

TREASURE GUIDE

Santa Cruz County—Time and the elements have all but obliterated all traces of the old mission of San Gabriel de Guevavi, the first church erected in Arizona by Europeans. All that remains of Guevavi are the remnants of a rapidly crumbling wall, a few trampled graves and a pile or two of weed-covered trash. These, too, may be gone by this time.

Guevavi served at first as the main mission and Tumacacori, to the north, as a visita. Sometime before 1764—the exact date is not known—Guevavi was abandoned in favor of Tumacacori, probably because of the threat of Apache raids in its isolated location.

However, before withdrawing from Guevavi, the black-robed priests are said to have buried the treasure taken from a nearby mine, together with the silver bells of the church and all the church ornaments. These were all placed in a secret hiding spot near the mission where they are said to remain to this day. It is hard to explain why the treasure was not transported the short distance of nine miles to Tumacacori.

In support of the story that the Guevavi padres had a mine which their Indian charges worked, is the statement that the remains of 16 **arrastres** were uncovered in the vicinity of Guevavi. The earliest American settlers in the southern Santa Cruz County are said to have found pieces of slag at the old mission ruins, and some are said to have realized a profit by shipping this slag to a smelter.

In modern times it is said that an old woodchopper named Juan Bustamente roamed the mountains on prospecting trips during the hot summer months when there was no demand for his wood in Nogales. He frequently brought in small quantities of fine gold dust, but one day he arrived at an assay office with two burros loaded with rich silver ore. No amount of persuasion would induce him to reveal where the ore had been secured. However, he did at a later date take a friend into his confidence and the two packed further quantities of rich ore into the border town.

It is believed that Bustamente had found the long-lost Guevavi Mission mine in the San Cayetano Mountains. He said that he had come upon an old wooden cross and near it had uncovered the entrance to an old mine tunnel. Investigation proved this to still be rich in unmined ore, the source of the silver he traded in Nogales. While visiting at Tumacacori one day a great cloudburst swept the San Cayetanos and he was never again able to locate the mine.

Santa Cruz County—Pete Kitchen was a retired soldier when he carved his ranch out of the very heart of the Apache empire. Located on the bandit and Indian-infested road from Magdalena, Sonora, to Tucson, Kitchen built a stronghold for his family, his workers and for any travelers passing that way. When other Americans fled the warring redskins, Kitchen stayed and defied the fierce Apaches to drive him out. The ranch was an armed camp and Kitchen called the road that passed his door, "Tucson, Tubac, Tumacacori and To Hell," the latter place being the destination of travelers caught by the Indians between stops.

Kitchen died in 1895 after carving out an enduring monument to himself as Arizona's "first and last pioneer," but his ranch still stands and is open to the public as a museum of the early Spanish era and the Old West. Today it is owned by Col. Gil Proctor, who has done a lot of research into every phase of history connected with the ranch.

One day an aged Mexican woman and two men approached Proctor and asked his permission to search for buried treasure. They had an electronic locating device and seemed very anxious to get on with the digging. Proctor agreed to the search provided they would tell him what they were looking for, and for a fifty percent share of anything they might find. They agreed, and this is the story the old Mexican woman told him.

When she was about 11 years of age, she had been employed to care for an aged Mexican woman who had lived on the ranch in the original adobe house. She had been there several weeks when she was told that her services were no longer needed. She was about ready to leave when the old woman asked her to assist in digging up a lard can. The two went into the yard and beneath the limbs of a tree they dug up a large can which was carried into the old woman's room and placed back of her bed. The woman told the young girl that it contained $20,000, the proceeds from the sale of her cattle over a period of years.

Some time later the girl was again summoned to the ranch to care for the old lady. Again she saw the lard can in the bedroom. Her services concluded, she returned to Nogales where she later heard that the old woman had died. Before her death, however, she had again buried the can of money under the tree. Her sons had searched for the treasure but failed to find it. Finally, they approached the girl, now grown to an old woman, and asked for her assistance in locating their mother's fortune. That is what had brought them to see Col. Proctor.

The search lasted for several days as the detector was taken from tree to tree, into the old adobe shack and generally through the yard. Nothing was found.

At a later date, a second woman approached Proctor with the story that her father had once worked for Pete Kitchen. Shortly before her father's death, she related, he had told her of 40,000 pesos he had buried on the ranch, the proceeds from the sale of cattle. A search was made, but with the same negative results. Other treasures are said to be buried on the old Kitchen Ranch, now owned by Col. Gil Proctor, who, if properly approached, seems to be agreeable to treasure hunting.

Santa Cruz County—Some 200 years ago, so the old Apache told Gil Proctor, his people lived at Las Lagunas, early name for the Pete Kitchen Ranch site. They raided the burro trains that passed through the region with loads of gold and silver bound for Mexico. The Apache raiders, according to the old Indian, had no use for the treasure stolen from the pack trains so they accumulated it and buried it under a white rock—Piedra Blanca. At the rancheria of Las Lagunas, the Indians laid out a large arrow made of rocks, and this pointed to the distant Piedra Blanca.

One day Spanish soldiers arrived at Las Lagunas and wiped out the settlement in retaliation for the raids. Only three Apaches managed to escape —and only these three knew the secret hiding place of the stolen gold. The Spanish never caught up with any of these three men and the treasure was never recovered.

One day Proctor stumbled upon a rock arrow right in his front yard! The rocks were so large and spaced so far apart that he never noticed that they were actually placed there in the form of a huge arrow. Two smaller rocks with a large rock in the center formed the point. Proctor set an Indian digging under the center rock and they found charcoal ("carbon" to the Spanish). Proctor knew that in the early Spanish days in America, charcoal was said to have been a sign for gold, and used in marking the site of buried gold.

Proctor took a compass bearing from the large rock forming the point of the arrow and followed it for a few miles. It brought him to no white rock. Perhaps he did not go far enough. Perhaps the rock is now covered.

Santa Cruz County—Legend has it that the mission padres of Tumacacori worked several gold and silver mines—now all lost. One of these mines was supposed to have been located in the foothills of the San Cayetano Mountains. It is pointed out that the original mission of San Jose del Tumacacori was known as San Cayetano de Tumacacori, and that the mine was named after it. The mine became lost after an Apache raid in 1722.

Another Tumacacori Mission mine was the La Virgen de Guadalupe supposed to have been located in the Santa Rita Mountains. An old Spanish document is said to have stated that upon approaching the mine a rock would be found on which would be carved the symbol CCB/TD. South of this rock a short distance would be found a small monument of rocks directly over the mine entrance which was covered with tons of earth to conceal it. An old legend of the Papago Indians says that a vast amount of gold and silver taken from the Guadalupe was hidden in its tunnel before it was sealed during the Apache troubles.

The original Tumacacori Mission stood on the west bank of the Santa Cruz River, while the present mission is on its east bank. An old Papago legend states that when the mission was abandoned, the gold and silver mined and stored in the Tumacacori mines was brought to the mission and concealed in the tunnel which ran from the original mission to the Santa Cruz River. No trace of the tunnel has ever been found.

When Tumacacori Mission stood abandoned, it was rapidly falling into ruins at the hands of treasure seekers who were literally tearing it apart. So far as it is known, nothing of value was ever found. The National Park

Service, in restoring the mission, made extensive excavations and investigations. They emphatically denied that any treasure of any kind was ever found. Nor do authorities agree upon the extent of mining activities carried on by Tumacacori's mission padres.

Santa Cruz County—The Opata Indians are now almost extinct, their demise hastened by the Spanish masters they so despised. Unlike their tractable neighbors, the Papagos, the Opatas regarded the Spanish as trespassers from the very start and carried a deep resentment against the forced labor to which they were subjected.

Grudgingly submissive, and only pretending to accept Christianity under the mission system, the Opatas clung to their own pagan religion and secretly kept alive their traditional tribal rites and ceremonies.

The Opatas were forced to work in several Spanish mission mines. The fact that their overseers wore the robes of the Church and carried crosses made little difference to them. They hated the Spanish whether they were soldiers or priests—and they hated the mines. There was one silver mine, however, which they worked diligently, and this the padres could not understand. Why did they make trouble at all the mines except this one? They called it the Opata Mine.

The silver ore in the Opata Mine, supposedly located near the Mexican border due south of the present Tumacacori Mission, was reached through a tunnel in the side of a mountain. The ore was brought out, crushed in *arrastres* and cast into bars. These were taken back into the mine where they were stored in a cave-like room at the furthest end of the tunnel. With the Indians in the Opata Mine working in apparent contentment, it was seldom necessary for the padres to enter the mine except for an occasional check. What they did not know was that the large underground chamber was a secret tribal meeting place, and this explained their strange good behavior.

The Opatas had been brought to Arizona from Sonora where they had been unfriendly neighbors of the Mayo tribe. In a mystery that has never been solved, the Mayos had among their numbers certain tribal members with almost white skin, blue eyes and blonde hair. The females of fair skin were looked upon with great favor and tribal veneration.

The Opatas had seen these blonde women and regarded the tribe with envy and jealousy. The Opatas working in the Opata mine determined to have a blonde Mayo woman as goddess of their own clan, and sent a party of males to the Mayo country to kidnap one. In due time they arrived back at the Opata's mine with the daughter of a powerful chief.

Kept a prisoner in the mine with the great hoard of silver bars, the blonde Mayo maiden was worshipped and given everything she desired except her freedom. She participated in their ritual functions and became their virtual leader. But she was not an Opata, and to bind her stronger to the tribe, it was agreed that she should wed the tribal leader. This she refused to do and no amount of persuasion or threats would make her change her mind. At length the frustrated Opatas decided to sacrifice the obstinate Mayo female to their pagan gods, and arrangements were made to carry out the ceremony in their underground chamber. The girl screamed, cried and shouted. She brought the curse of her people upon her captors.

In the quiet of a peaceful Sabbath morning outside the mine, a passing padre paused to listen to the strange noises coming from the mine tunnel. He entered cautiously and heard the last dying moans of the murdered Mayo woman. When he arrived at her side she was dead. He ordered the Opatas from the mine.

That day the padres summoned the Opatas together and told them to prepare to return to Sonora. There was great rejoicing. They had lost the blonde Mayo woman, but they had regained their freedom.

Remorseful over their neglect to watch the Opata miners closer, the padres decided that the fortune stored in the mine should never be used. They called in their faithful charges, the Papagos, and ordered them to fill in the mine tunnel, conceal the entrance and close the Opata Mine forever. When their work was done the mine was abandoned and to this day no trace of it has ever been found.

Santa Cruz County—John Ward came to Arizona from San Francisco by way of Mexico at an early date. Although little is known of his early life, it was commonly thought that he had left California just one step ahead of the vigilantes. Settling in an old house just west of the town of Patagonia, Ward married a Mexican woman who had a son by a previous marriage.

In 1860 the son was kidnapped by Apaches and the blame was placed on Chief Cochise who bitterly denied the act. During the raid on his place, Ward is said to have buried valuables of unknown value and description. It was believed that Ward had either brought the wealth to Arizona with him or that he had found the hidden wealth of one of the early California missions. No explanation is given as to why Ward never recovered his treasure, but the legend has persisted throughout the years that the wealth is still buried and there has been much digging for it.

Yavapai County—George R. Casner brought a herd of sheep from California into Arizona in 1876 and established a ranch near what is now called Casner Mountain about 25 miles southwest of Flagstaff and just south of the Yavapai-Coconino county line. As time passed, he disposed of his sheep and bought cattle. Around Flagstaff and throughout the Verde Valley he was reputed to be a wealthy man, having brought a sizeable fortune with him from California. It is said that he always dealt in gold, and expected to be paid in gold when he sold his herds. It was known that he never used banks.

After Casner arrived home from a selling trip, a cowboy working for him noted that he always disappeared for a day or two, and that two augers hanging in the barn always disappeared with him. When these were replaced, they were bright and shiny, indicating that they had recently been used. It was later learned that Casner had devised a method of hiding his gold by boring holes in pine trees near his ranch. After placing $1,000 in each hole, a neatly carved plug concealed the spot from prying eyes.

One day Casner informed his lone cowhand that he had enough money to retire, and that he was going to return to California. Later the cowboy learned that Casner had shipped only a small amount of gold by express from Flagstaff. It was immediately assumed that he had been unable to locate the trees in which the major part of his fortune had been hidden, and that he had left without it.

In 1889 two cowboys accidentally found $1,000 in gold coins stuffed into a hole in a tree which had been felled by lightning. This revived stories of Casner's hidden wealth and repeated searches were made for trees containing his wealth. So far as it is known, nothing additional was ever found.

Yavapai County—"Old Mose" Casner, of whom very little is known, operated a horse and cattle ranch in the reaches of Beaver Creek Canyon, near the town of Rimrock in northeastern Yavapai County. Casner is supposed to have accumulated a fortune of $100,000 which he buried on his ranch in five dutch ovens, each containing $20,000 in gold coins, and each buried in a separate location. It was Casner's theory that a party finding one of the treasures would think that he had all of it and leave. It is said that Casner died a natural death, never revealing where his dutch ovens were buried.

So far as we can determine Old Mose Casner's treasure has never been verified, and it is our opinion that the story stems from the George R. Casner treasure. It is interesting to note, in relation to the above two stories, that a John Casner treasure story, similar in several details to the above, is placed in Palo Duro Canyon in Texas.

Yavapai County—Horsethief Basin is a small open area on the east side of Lane Mountain in the colorful Bradshaw Mountains north of Phoenix. For many years in the early history of the region, there was a ranch located here which was known as Horsethief Ranch or Horse Mesa Ranch, after the several noted characters who operated it as a hideout for their stolen horses.

The first cabin built here was erected by a rustler known as Horsethief Davis. He was later joined by a pal who had the nickname of Horsethief Thompson. In their day the old Horsethief Trail from Utah to Mexico passed through here, and the basin was used as a stopover point. Animals stolen in the Salt River Valley could be quickly smuggled into the natural basin, its high slopes on every side making it a perfect hiding place. All entrances into the basin could be guarded by a few men and an alarm sounded at the approach of strangers.

Here, too, all brands were appropriately altered. Animals stolen in the

Salt River region were then driven to Prescott and sold, while the return trip was made with horses stolen around Prescott and sold in the Salt River Valley. This two-way traffic in stolen animals worked well until the country around Horsethief Basin attracted settlers, thereby destroying the isolation the thieves required for their safety. They then moved out.

In 1939 the cabin in which the outlaws had lived was moved to another site. Its earth floor had been thoroughly dug up by treasure seekers searching for the money persistent rumors said was buried there. If any was ever found, it never came to public light. The City of Phoenix leased 4,000 acres here in 1936 from the U. S. Forest Service, and today Horsethief Basin is a popular summer camp and recreational area.

Yavapai County—A half century has passed since two aged Mexican brothers stopped at a ranch south of the Black Canyon country. They were loaded down with mining equipment and had provisions for a prolonged stay. They had come north from Mexico, they said, at the insistence of their mother, then past 90 years of age, to search for a placer deposit once worked by their father, now dead.

The placer was located on a high black mesa overlooking a rugged canyon. Their father had taken a burro load of gold from the place before being forced to leave by Indians. But he had managed to make a map of the place and the brothers had it with them.

Studying the waybill carefully, the rancher finally directed the Mexicans to a black lava-strewn mesa on the west side of Black Canyon. With gracious thanks the next morning, the brothers departed in high hopes. They found a mesa such as the rancher had described, but after days of fruitless search they gave up and returned to the ranch where they stayed overnight. On the following morning they took off for Mexico, leaving the map with the rancher.

The rancher all but forgot the incident. Then it suddenly occurred to him that he had noted some signs of placer mining while riding on the mesa several years previously. He had not paused to investigate, but now he thought it worth looking into. After a week's search of the mesa he concluded that the Indians, after driving the Mexican brothers out of the area, had covered the placer to conceal it from view, and that a cloudburst had washed away the cover. A later storm, he figured, had again concealed all sign of the black mesa placer.

The area of the mesa is generally believed to be in the vicinity of Rock Springs on the Black Canyon Highway (Interstate 17).

Yavapai County—The town of Gillette, founded in 1870 as the mill town for the famed Tip Top Mine and others, is now a ghost of crumbled foundations almost covered by a growth of trees. The area was the scene of many stage holdups during its boom days and there are several stories of buried treasure in the vicinity.

Within a short span of time in 1882, a lone masked bandit committed three stage robberies on the outskirts of Gillette, securing a total of $69,000. Officers were unable to track the bandit after any of the robberies, and the incidents remained a mystery until suspicion was cast upon a Gillette blacksmith named Henry Seymour.

Setting a trap for the holdup man, the town marshal, Henry Garfias, caught Seymour in the act of committing his fourth holdup. Seymour stubbornly refused to talk, even when sentenced to a 10-year term in the Territorial Prison at Yuma. A search of his cabin and the area where the holdups had been committed failed to turn up any loot. When Seymour was released from prison, he dropped from sight and is not known to have returned to Gillette in an attempt to recover the treasure he is believed to have left there.

Yavapai County—Byron D. P. Duppa, a native of England, settled in the Salt River Valley in 1863. Very little is known of his background, but he is thought to have been a British army officer who left the service following a duel with a fellow officer. His receipt of $12,000 annually from England would indicate a wealthy and perhaps titled parentage. His title of "Lord" seems to have been self-imposed.

For a time Duppa ran the stage station at Agua Fria, where he later operated a ranch. Some looked upon him as a worthless snob, while others saw him as a man of education and refinement. No matter which, he left his mark on Arizona history for it was he who suggested the names for the present cities of Phoenix and Tempe.

There was talk in Arizona that Duppa had a silver mine somewhere in the Bradshaw Mountains. The ledge was said to have been found in partnership with Andrew Starar, a neighboring rancher, while the two were trying to prove to themselves that any man could find a mine if old Jacob Walz could. Both Starar and Duppa were well aware of Walz's famed Lost Dutchman Mine. After finding their mine, both Duppa and Starar are said to have lost interest in it almost immediately—Duppa because his remittance from England was more than enough to keep him comfortably, and Starar because his ranch provided enough income to keep him in whiskey.

In 1872 Duppa was badly wounded by Apaches at his Agua Fria ranch. Although it was a few years before he passed on, it is claimed that both he and Starar died without ever revealing the location of their silver mine in the Bradshaws.

Yavapai County—Sometime during the late 1880's a priest appeared in Prescott seeking assistance in locating some buried gold. He related that a dying man in a Denver hospital had told him that he and two partners had taken $75,000 worth of gold from a placer mine in Navajo County on northeastern Arizona. It was an area jealously guarded by the Indians, and fearing an attack, they took their gold and fled east into New Mexico. From here they traveled south before again turning west into Arizona. Along the way two of the partners died, leaving the sole survivor with the gold. Following the Gila and Verde rivers to the vicinity of Camp Verde, the lone survivor turned westward, finally reaching the mountainous country just south of Prescott. Here he was surprised by a band of Indians, and in order to facilitate his escape, he buried the gold under a boulder along a stream at the base of a mountain. When he reached Prescott he was broken of health and abandoned all thought of recovering the gold until a later date. Making his way to friends in Denver, he was hospitalized. Here he met the priest, and when he was about to die, passed the secret of the buried gold on to him. It was never found.

Yavapai County—In 1905 a cowboy named Chalmer Harper was employed on the Perrin Land and Cattle Company ranch some 50 miles northwest of Prescott. While stationed at a remote line camp at the foot of Dairy Mountain, he became ill and companions persuaded him to ride to Prescott to consult a doctor. Setting out alone, he passed through Camp Wood, but by the time he reached Smith Canyon he was so weak that he stopped for a rest. While reclining in the shade of a large boulder, a deer emerged from nearby bushes. Harper reached for his rifle and shot it, making a meal of some of the venison.

Feeling revived, the cowboy decided to move on. As he arose from his resting place, the heel of his boot dislodged a rock that caught his attention. He inspected it and found that it contained flecks of gold. Digging further, he uncovered a pocket of rich ore. Harper gathered all the ore he could carry and carefully concealed the spot with earth and brush. To mark the spot, he beheaded the dead deer and hung the head and antlers in the branches of a juniper tree. On the following day Harper reached a ranch at Iron Springs where he collapsed. The rancher took him to a doctor in Prescott in a wagon.

Upon being advised that he was in the advanced stages of tuberculosis and had not long to live, Harper had the doctor summon his brother from Texas. When the brother arrived in Prescott, the dying cowboy told him of his discovery in Smith Canyon. After his brother's death, Henry Harper had an assay made of the samples his brother had brought to Prescott. They were so rich they paid the dead man's hospital and funeral expenses.

In time, Henry Harper organized a small expedition and went in search of the juniper tree with a deer's skull and antlers hanging in it. A thorough search of Smith Canyon failed to reveal it. In the belief that the dead man might have been mistaken in the name of the canyon, other nearby canyons were searched. Failing, the party disbanded and Henry Harper returned to Texas. So far as it is known, Chalmer Harper's mine has never been found.

Yavapai County—One day two prospectors observed an Apache trading gold nuggets for supplies in the post at Fort McDowell. It was known that the Indian lived in the Bronco Canyon region on the Fort Apache Indian Reservation, and it was assumed that his gold came from this area. Determined to have a go at finding the Apache's gold, and knowing that it would be useless to try to follow him, the two prospectors outfitted themselves for a prolonged search.

Establishing their camp near a spring in Bronco Caynon, the two prospectors ranged out in systematic fashion day after day, careful that they were not seen by the Apaches. And then they struck a rich vein of gold-filled quartz!

It was partially covered with brush and showed signs of being worked recently. Whether it was the Apache's source of gold or not didn't matter. It was rich, and it was theirs as long as the Apaches did not find them. By the time winter closed their operation, they had a moderate fortune—and plans for the spring.

Resuming mining with the opening of spring weather, the prospectors constructed a crude **arrastre** and shortly produced between $70,000 and $80,000 worth of gold. This wealth was stored temporarily under a huge rock near the camp where it would stay until fall, Then it would be packed out to San Francisco where they could purchase badly needed equipment to increase their production.

On the morning of their planned departure for the winter, a party of Apaches crept down upon the miners and opened fire without warning. One of the men fell dead just as he struck his pick into the ground. The other managed to reach his rifle and scamper to concealment behind a boulder. Crawling through the tangled brush, he made his escape.

Having had the fright of his life, and realizing how lucky he had been in evading death, the lone surviving miner decided not to return to the mine until the Indians were completely subdued. He was in his eighties when he thought this time had arrived. Stopping off in Phoenix on his way to the mine, he became ill and was hospitalized. Before he died, he told the story of the mine for the first time.

Several years later a Mexican sheepherder told of finding a rusty pick sticking in the ground in Bronco Canyon. He knew nothing of its significance. Others have reported seeing the remains of a crude **arrastre** in the same region, but the mine is said never to have been found.

Yavapai County—In 1862, Major Abraham H. Peeples was prospecting and mining at La Paz and other points along the Colorado River. Indians inhabiting the mountain regions came to La Paz to make purchases from the white traders, paying for their merchandise with gold which they seemed to have in unlimited quantities. When white men tried to bribe the Indians to tell where the gold came from, they were told that a tribal oath prevented the Indians from telling.

Major Peeples finally gained the confidence of a young Apache, and in exchange for a number of mules, he agreed to meet Peeples at a secret rendezvous and take him to the gold. The Indian failed to show up. Under the pressure of additional bribes, the Indian later took Peeples, Jack Swilling and a couple of other white men into the mountains. Around the campfire one night the Indian said they were near the gold, which was scattered over the floor of a small canyon. By morning the Indian was gone and they never saw him again.

Peeples and his disappointed party decided to push on into the mountains indicated by the missing Apache, careful that they did not stumble into an ambush. On the third morning in the mountains, the Mexican charged with taking care of the party's horses and mules found they had strayed during the night. Climbing a hill to get a better view of the surrounding country, the Mexican came upon a slight depression that was literally carpeted with nuggets and slugs of native gold, He picked up several of the larger nuggets, rounded up the straying animals, and returned to the camp where he displayed his find. Excitedly, the men moved to the top of the hill—and there was the gold just as the Mexican had said. Nuggets worth $500 and $600 were picked up with ease, and in a short time each man in the party had gathered a considerable fortune.

That hill became known as Rich Hill, visible today to one's right while traveling northeast on US 89 between Congress Junction and Peeples Valley. Before its riches played out, it had produced a total of $70,000,000! Major Peeples had found riches enough for any man, but he was still intrigued as to the whereabouts of the small canyon whose floor was covered with gold as described to him by the young Apache. For several years he kept parties searching for the Lost Apache Mine.

Yavapai County—Negro Ben was a hand on the Major Peeples ranch in Peeples Valley. It was a region where rich strikes were common, and Negro Ben frequently made his own little prospecting trips into the surrounding hills, much to the annoyance of his employer.

After the great find at Rich Hill, local Indians laughed at the white man's greed for gold and taunted them with statements that they knew where here was a much greater field of gold on Big Antelope, a name then familiar only to the Indians.

Traditionally, the Indians held the black man in some kind of awe, and it has been said that a Negro could often pass unharmed through the most hostile Indian country. Perhaps it is not so strange that Negro Ben made friends with several Yavapai chiefs, and in particular with an old Apache who loafed around the Peeples ranch. From this Indian, Negro Ben heard the story of the Big Antelope gold.

After some slight persuasion, Negro Ben induced the old Apache to take him to Big Antelope. Secretly they started out together, but at Sycamore Springs the Apache stopped and refused to go another step. "It is near," he said, and that is all Negro Ben could get out of him.

Negro Ben searched the area for three days before returning to the ranch in disgust. Gold fever had him, however, and before long he deserted his job and disappeared into the hills. The next time Major Peeples saw him he was hanging around Wickenburg, apparently in possession of enough gold to remain in a constant state of intoxication. When he went broke, he simply slipped away in the night and returned in a few days with his burro loaded with rich gold ore which he washed out at the river.

Although Negro Ben was closely watched, he was too cunning to be followed. His usual trip took him westward to the Harquahala Mountains, and he always returned from the same direction, but it was assumed that this was only a ruse to confuse his pursuers. Major Peeples did not believe that his short absence from Wickenburg allowed him sufficient time to make a round trip to the Harquahalas, and he figured that Negro Ben headed north to shake off any followers.

One day Negro Ben did not return from his periodic trip in the usual period of time. When he was overdue several days there was some concern for his safety. Finally a search party was formed and in due time his body was found. The location of the body could be a clue as to the location of the mine, if he had one, but accounts do not agree. The Florence (Ariz.) **Tribune** stated that the Negro's body was found four miles west of Wickenburg, and that he had undoubtedly been slain by Apaches because they had been suspicious of his color! It seems more likely that the Apaches figured that sooner or later a white man would succeed in following Negro Ben, and then would come others to disturb the peace of Big Antelope, which they held in some kind of reverence.

The theory was presented that Negro Ben's mine was in the vicinity of Oro Grande, north of Wickenburg. The Phoenix **Republican** reported in 1890 that the mine was in the vicinity of McCracken, which was in agreement with Peeples' belief. But the popular location of Negro Ben's mine was near Antelope Peak at the southern end of Peeples Valley, northeast of Wickenburg.

Both Major Peeples and Ed Schieffelin made extensive searches for Negro Ben's gold, and in the years that followed, many others sought the source of the rich ore that kept the Negro in whiskey. "He was a good man, even if his skin was black," said Peeples, and he had Negro Ben's body taken to his ranch and buried.

Yuma County—William B. Rood came to California in 1849 with the ill-fated "Jayhawkers" party from Illinois, and was one of the survivors of the terrible Death Valley crossing. When Pauline Weaver made his sensational discovery of gold near the Colorado River above Yuma in 1862, Rood followed the rush to the booming town of La Paz. He prospected and ranched, selecting a site on the east bank of the Colorado about midway between La Paz and Yuma. To this ranch he gave the name of Rancho de los Yumas. He prospered by supplying beef to the several army posts in the region, becoming a substantial and respectable citizen.

TREASURE GUIDE

In April, 1870, Rood and his foreman, Alex Poindexter, crossed the Colorado in a small boat to pay his Indian woodchoppers. Poindexter returned to the ranch and reported that Rood had drowned when the craft struck a snag and capsized. There were those who suspected that Poindexter had murdered Rood in order to find the wealth the rancher was rumored to have hidden around his home at Rancho de los Yumas.

When William Rood's estate was settled, the public administrator could find no money except a few hundred dollars on deposit with merchants in Yuma, a common custom in settlements where no banks were available. From all of Rood's many and profitable enterprises, it was believed that he had accumulated a sizeable fortune. He was known to have kept gold at his ranch, and it was concluded that he had buried the major portion of his wealth.

It is stated upon good authority that both Poindexter and his wife searched Rancho de los Yumas after Rood's death. At the time of his death, Rood had two daughters in a convent in Los Angeles. They, too, are said to have made many searches for their father's wealth, but without success.

After the death of Rood, Rancho de los Yumas rapidly fell into ruins, used by travelers as an overnight stopping place, and searched over by many people who passed that way. In 1897, Alfredo Pina, a Mexican woodcutter, dug an old baking powder tin from its crumbling walls and recovered about $1,000 in gold coins. He found papers, too, but unable to read them, threw them away. Some believe these papers may have contained directions to the burial place of Rood's major treasure.

Under the assault of many treasure seekers, and compounded by the ravages of time and the elements, the last of the adobe walls of Rancho de los Yumas are rapidly disappearing into the desert. There is strong reason to believe that this treasure actually exists, unless, of course, it has been found and not reported. What remains of the old ranch buildings can still be located.

Yuma County—Many years ago, when an epidemic of cholera hit northern Sonora, Mexico, a young Mexican girl and a Papago Indian boy were left homeless and without relatives. The boy suggested to the girl that she go with him to Gila City, Arizona (now only a site on the Gila River east of Yuma), where he had some distant relatives they could live with. She agreed to accompany him and they traveled afoot across the waterless stretches of the Camino del Diablo, an awesome stretch of desert road that had claimed hundreds of lives. At the base of the Cabeza Prieta Mountains of Yuma County, the girl became so weak from lack of water that she could no longer go on. The young Indian placed her in the shade of a rock and went in search of water.

In the lower reaches of the mountains the boy found a tank, a natural depression that holds water until it evaporates. Somehow he managed to take some of it to the suffering girl. When she was able to be moved they made their way to the tank where they planned to stay until the girl regained her strength. It is believed that this tank was the one now known as Tule Well.

When they were ready to leave, the Papago boy led the girl up an arroyo and on to the top of a granite mesa, where there was a small stream visible a short distance below. The boy told the girl to look down. In the clear water of the stream was a layer of gold nuggets, as if the stream bed had been paved with them. Before resuming their journey, the boy gathered some of the nuggets, and eventually they arrived in Gila City where the pair was taken in by his relatives.

After the passing of a few years, the Mexican girl married an American named George Whistler, and she showed him some of the nuggets which she still had in her possession. Before Whistler got around to searching for the stream in the Cabeza Prietas, he was killed in a fight. Upon his promise to share anything found, the girl gave the secret to a friend, Tom Childs. He and others searched for the gold-laden stream, but nothing was found. They decided that the stream had been filled with debris shaken down by an earthquake, or that a sudden cloudburst had changed its course.

Yuma County—On his way to the California gold fields, "Doctor" Able B. Lincoln, after serving in the Mexican War, stopped over at Yuma Crossing (now Yuma, Arizona), where it was necessary to be ferried across the Colorado River by one of two ferries operating there. Lincoln immediately saw the money to be made at Yuma and purchased one of the ferries. In his first three months of operation, Lincoln's ferry, in his own words, grossed more than $60,000. "But," Lincoln wrote to his people in the east, "this place is unsafe to live in and I plan to leave in a few months."

John Glanton had also served in the Mexican War, where he earned a bad reputation. Later he became a professional scalp hunter for the Mexican government, being paid $50 to $100 for each Apache scalp he brought in. When Glanton ran out of Apaches to scalp, he killed Mexicans, trimmed their scalps to look like Apaches, and collected the bounty on these. When the Mexicans got wise to this, he fled the country in a hurry.

At Yuma Crossing, Glanton met Able Lincoln and somehow managed to muscle in on Lincoln's lucrative ferry business. On the side, Glanton robbed California-bound gold seekers, killed them if they resisted and dumped their bodies into the Colorado. Deciding to put the second ferry—it was operated by Indians—out of business, Glanton cut the craft loose at night and it drifted helplessly down the river. In retaliation, the Indians waited their chance and attacked the whites in force as they slept one night. Glanton's head was chopped off and Lincoln was clubbed to death.

One of the three ferrymen to escape the attack said later that Lincoln had $50,000 in silver and between $20,000 and $30,000 in gold which he kept buried someplace near his camp. Glanton is believed to have had a similar fortune which he is believed to have buried in the thickets on the west bank of the river, placing it in California. The rampaging Indians are believed to have discovered a small part of the treasure, probably no more than $5,000, which had not yet been buried. After the massacre of the Yuma ferrymen at Yuma Crossing, an area then claimed by the State of California, Governor Burnett of California ordered an expedition of 142 men to Yuma Crossing to protect travelers, to punish the Indians, and to recover the treasure hidden by Lincoln and Glanton. The Gila Expedition, as the California military party was called, consumed an incredible four years. Nobody was punished and absolutely nothing was accomplished. The expedition cost the State of California $113,482.25, which was more than the state treasury held at that time. They did not find the buried gold and silver.

Yuma County—John Nummel died in 1948, so the memory of his lost mine in the Chocolate Mountains north of Yuma is still fresh in the minds of a lot of people. He had come to Arizona from Germany in the late 1870's or early 1880's, and worked in several of the mines in southwestern Yuma County, walking across the hot desert from one to another when he did not have a burro.

Nummel often worked for the Red Cloud Mine along the Colorado River above Picacho, and for the La Fortuna Mine on the western slopes of the Gila Mountains southeast of Yuma. As he followed the old Red Cloud-Fortuna trail between the two mines, he prospected along the way, frequently straying many miles from the trail.

Sometime between 1895 and 1900, Nummel left the employ of the Red Cloud and started on the long walk to the Fortuna. It was a distance of about 40 miles and there was little trail to follow. Someplace before reaching his goal, Nummel sat down to rest in the skimpy patch of shade cast by a palo verde tree. From pure habit, he took his hammer and broke off a piece of a nearby ledge. To his amazement, it was richly colored with free gold. Without tools or supplies he could not immediately take advantage of his find, and he did not want to return to the Red Cloud for he had quit in a huff.

Pocketing a piece of the ore, he proceeded to the La Fortuna, determined to take a job there and save enough money to develop his find. Before long, however, he had a disagreement with the La Fortuna foreman and started the long trek back to the Red Cloud, planning to investigate the ledge a second time. He could not locate a single familiar landmark. In a region that he had tramped many times, everything seemed to have changed. He could not explain it.

Between jobs to keep in provisions and supplies, Nummel searched for the lost ledge. He swore he could see that ledge just as it was—the tree and the rocks he had built into a mound to mark the place. Up until the very last years of his life, he never gave up—and he never succeeded. John

ARIZONA

Nummel's lost ledge of gold is still to be found.

Yuma County—James Hurley was grubstaked by a Parker, Arizona, storekeeper and instructed to prospect the area around Black Mountain to the southeast. On his first day out, Hurley came across an old wagon half buried in the sand behind some desert vegetation. It offered a good place to make camp so he stopped for the night.

On the ground near the wagon, and almost covered with drifted sand, was the body of a man, almost reduced to a skeleton. His curiosity aroused, Hurley turned his attention to the wagon. Scooping out some of the sand, he uncovered a half-rotted tarpaulin. Underneath this he recovered 15 rotted sacks of rich gold-bearing ore of a peculiar color he had never seen before. He packed as much of the ore as he could carry and took it to Parker, where it smelted out $1,800 worth of gold.

Hurley returned to the wagon immediately with the intention of tracking the ore to its source. But the wagon had been there quite a period of time and standstorms had covered its trail. He could no more than guess at its last course. For the next five years Hurley searched the surrounding area in all directions, but he could find nothing that even remotely resembled the peculiar color of the ore. Nor could he later find any old prospector who had ever seen anything like it. Where had it come from? How far had the wagon traveled since it had been loaded? Hurley could solve neither riddle, but he died believing that Black Mountain held the answer.

Yuma County—The first copper mine worked in Arizona by Americans is claimed to have been the Planet, discovered by a man named Hyland in 1863, near Planet Peak in the Buckskin Mountains. One day the owner or superintendent of the Planet left the mine to escort a party of eastern stockholders to the stage station at Quartzsite. His mission ended, he was on his way back to the Planet when he was caught in a whipping sandstorm that blackened out the sun.

Completely lost and wandering aimlessly for several days, the man settled down to rest by a ledge of rock that protruded from the sand. Curling up at the base of the ledge, he pulled his coat up over his head, wondering if the storm would ever abate, and if he would have the strength to go on if it did.

When the storm finally blew itself out and he struggled to regain his feet, he noticed that the ledge was quartz and that it was sprinkled with free gold. He broke off a few pieces and placed them in his pack. Then he made a written description of the surrounding landmarks, and in order to mark the place for easy finding when he returned, he took off his two six-shooters and left them on the ledge.

Heading his weakened horse in what he supposed was the direction of the Planet mine, he slumped into the saddle and tried to hold on. When the horse appeared at the mining settlement without its rider, a search party left immediately to find the missing mining man. His body was found on the desert in the general area of Bouse. In his pack was found the samples he had taken from the ledge, and notes describing its location. When the ore was assayed it showed $25,000 to the ton. But the Lost Six-Shooter Mine has never been found.

Yuma County—It was a black winter night when a miner named Billy Orme stumbled into the stage station at Culling's Well, guided there by a lighted lantern hung from a tall pole. Orme had been in Ehrenberg securing supplies and was on his way back to meet his partner, Jacob Hamlin, at the Bullard Mine in the Harcuvar Mountains north of Aquila. When Joe Drew, the station keeper, saw Orme, he realized at once that Orme was so drunk he couldn't stand up. He was missing his six-shooter and his pockets were filled with heavy black rocks.

At first Orme couldn't even remember whether he had left Ehrenberg two days previously or three days. It was not until the following morning that he sobered up sufficiently to begin putting the pieces together. He told Drew that he had spent one night at the base of a ledge of black rock. Picking up a piece of the rock the following morning, he recognized it to be rich in native silver. The whole ledge was silver. It was a veritable bonanza!

The only other thing that Orme could recall of his trip was that he had placed his six-shooter at the base of the ledge and built a mound of rocks over it to mark the site. But he had no idea where the ledge was, except that it was some place between Ehrenberg and Culling's Well—a distance of 140 miles!

Orme and his partner spent many weary months searching patiently along the trails between the two points. When Hamlin gave up, Orme stayed on and continued the search for the remainder of his life.

Yuma County—In 1869 Abner McKeever and his family operated a ranch near the Big Bend of the Gila River, near the present town of Gila Bend. One day McKeever and his young daughter, Belle, were working on a small placer claim some distance from the protection of the ranch. For a moment the father relaxed his guard and a small band of Apaches swooped down from the hills and seized the pair. Letting the man go, they took the screaming girl and rode away to the north.

Pursuit without help was out of the question, and although it cost precious time, Abner rode with all possible speed to Fort Yuma where there was a garrison of soldiers. Soon they were riding to Gila Bend at full speed.

Sighting the approach of the soldiers, the Apaches broke into small bands and fled in different directions. Not knowing which band held the captive girl, the soldiers also divided and gave chase to all groups. In one of these detachments was a sergeant named Crossthwaite, and under him were two privates, Joe Wormley and Eugene Flannigan. The band of Indians they followed rapidly disappeared in a northwesterly direction. Soon they lost the Indians, and it wasn't long before they lost themselves in the rocky hills. It was a region noted for its lack of water.

First, the soldiers ran out of provisions. Then their horses dropped one by one of exhaustion. They struggled on afoot in a desperate search for water, the girl all but forgotten. Wormley became delirious and it was all his companions could do to keep him from wandering off by himself. All three were about to collapse when they came to a small spring in the Granite Wash Mountains of Northern Yuma County. That night they camped beside the spring and were fortunate to kill some small game on which they feasted. While washing in the spring the following morning, Crossthwaite was amazed to find some gold nuggets. The three men pocketed those that they could pick off the surface.

Knowing enough about prospecting to look for a vein or outcropping, the three soldiers turned their attention to the surrounding region. Above the spring, a short distance away, they located not one vein but two, one narrow and the other about 16 feet in width. With their knives they dug out about 50 pounds of the ore and headed south.

But the return journey was fraught with equal hardships. In a few days they were again delirious with thirst. Late that afternoon Crossthwaite was unable to stagger on and dropped by the wayside. Flannigan was next, and Wormley half-crawled and half-walked on alone. Eventually, he managed to reach the Gila River where he was rescued in the nick of time. From his almost hysterical babblings, the rescuers pieced together the story and raced off in search of Flannigan and Crossthwaite. When they found Flannigan, he was more dead than alive, but they managed to pull him through. Crossthwaite was dead.

When Flannigan and Wormley were fully recovered from their ordeal, they related the story in detail and gave directions as best they could for locating the rich veins of gold. Flannigan flatly refused to return to the area. He died in Phoenix in 1880. Wormley led several searches for the spring and the ledge of ore above it, but all were fruitless. Among the many who believed in the lost mine was Harold Bell Wright, the author, who is said to have sought it persistently.

The Belle McKeever Mine, so far as it is known, has never been found. And Belle McKeever was never found, but the search for the little girl was never as intensive as that for the gold.

Yuma County—When Don Jose Maria Redondo came to Arizona from Mexico, he already possessed a fortune made from various gold strikes, ferrying and other successful ventures. He laid out a vast estate about 15 miles north of Yuma. Most of the land he simply appropriated from the public domain. Here, in the Gila Valley, he built the Hacienda de San Ysidro, a self-sustaining empire employing as many as 300 workers. The massive two-story hacienda headquarters was made of mountains of adobe bricks. There were many outbuildings—a mill for grinding the grain Redondo grew, a winery to handle the products of his vinyards, cookhouses, warehouses, offices, blacksmith shop, harness shops, stables and corrals.

By 1871 Don Jose Redondo and his brother James had many stores in Yuma. Don Jose served in the Territorial Legislature, on the Yuma city council, and later became mayor of Yuma. But in 1874 government land surveyors came to Gila Valley and divided his vast estate into sections and townships. Finding it impossible to defend the title to his holdings, Redondo saw his vast estate reduced to a single section of land. In disgust he abandoned Hacienda de San Ysidro and moved to Yuma. Almost immediately San Ysidro fell victim to the ravages of neighbors and the destruction wrought by treasure hunters.

No one knows how the stories started that Don Jose had left a fortune buried or hidden at San Ysidro, nor is there any explanation why Redondo would move away from the estate under voluntary and peaceful circumstances and leave any wealth behind, but so extensive have been the searches for treasure that Hacienda de San Ysidro was rapidly reduced to ruins. Practically nothing is left of it today, and it is not known that any treasure was ever found.

Yuma County—Ed Schieffelin, one of Arizona's most noted—and successful—prospectors, after finding the great Tombstone bonanzas, spent many years in roaming around North America in search of another rich strike. One day in Yuma he heard of an old squaw who had found a very rich deposit of gold. Many had tried to pry the secret location from the old woman, but all had failed. Schieffelin decided to try his luck with her.

He located the squaw's hogan along the Colorado River and spent hours talking to her. When the conversation was over, he knew no more than before. He went to the hogan and talked to her again and again. Finally, she gave him a vague description of a place that could have been almost any spot in southwestern Arizona. She did say, however, that it was along the trail between Wickenbreg and Yuma. Schieffelin knew the country far too well to attempt any search in such a vast country. When the woman refused to define the area closer, Schieffelin gave up in disgust.

Next the squaw was approached by a small group of Mexican prospectors who had heard of the hidden deposit. When she refused to reveal anything to them, they applied some pressure. Still she would not talk. They threatened violence and went away, saying that they would be back. In the meantime the old squaw consulted her tribe. It was agreed that the Mexicans should be given some directions—false directions.

When the Mexicans returned, the squaw and two bucks offered to take them part way to the deposit. They left and traveled to the northern end of the Harquahala Mountains. Here she stopped and refused to go farther. The Mexicans beat her and when her tribesmen interceded, they were killed. Held a prisoner by the Mexicans, she resisted all efforts to force the secret from her. One night she managed to escape and returned to her

ARIZONA

people.

When an immensely rich strike was later made in the Harquahala Mountains, Ed Schieffelin visited the place and decided that this was the squaw's long lost deposit of gold. Others did not agree.

Yuma County—Among the many old mines supposedly once worked by the Spanish in Arizona, and later abandoned, was one known to the Yuma Indians because their ancestors had been slaves who worked in it. For many generations the secret location of the mine was handed down from fathers to sons, and the penalty for revealing its location was death. A few squaws presumably knew the secret.

An Englishman named Reginald Grey drifted into Yuma from the California gold fields and took up with the Yuma tribe. Eventually he married one of the squaws who held the secret of the old Spanish mine. When Grey learned of this he tried to pry its location from her, but her bonds with the tribe were strong and she refused.

One day the couple traveled Adonde Range and made camp at Bakers Tank. The squaw volunteered the information that they were near the old mine once worked by her people. When Grey asked her to show him its exact location, she refused because it was against tribal rules, but she did agree to go to the mine and bring out some of the ore while he remained at the camp. True to her word, the squaw left and when she returned she carried a sack of rich gold ore. Grey pressed her to return to the mine for another, and another. She obeyed and they returned to their village where the Englishman mortared out the gold.

Grey found this procedure to his liking and he kept the woman busy bringing ore to the village. One day she did not return after her allotted time and Grey became alarmed for her safety because he did not yet hold the secret of the mine's location. For weeks he searched for her without results, nor could he find her trail to the mine. Grey appealed to her people, but they denied all knowledge of her whereabouts. And they asked him to pack up and leave.

Legend avers that the squaw was killed by her own people, after which the entrance to the mine was completely obliterated.

Yuma County—An aged Mexican spent many months prospecting around the Castle Dome Range area north of Yuma. His failure was very discouraging. As he loafed at the old King of Arizona Mine one day, he decided that he had had enough. He loaded his burro and headed straight for Ehrenberg on the Colorado River.

In crossing a narrow gully, the old prospector noticed an outcropping that looked interesting. He broke off a piece of the ore, placed it in his pocket and trudged on.

Months later the old Mexican was in California, still carrying the piece of ore. Finally he got around to showing it to an assayer who pronounced it

93

TREASURE GUIDE

rich in gold. The two made a deal to look for the location, but before they got around to it, the aged Mexican died. Somewhere between the Kofa Mountains and the site of old Ehrenberg, the old Mexican's mine is presumably still waiting to be found.

Yuma County—There are several versions of this story, and all of them seem to be based on legend. According to the most popular version, three roughly dressed Frenchmen stopped their pack animals in front of Hooper & Company's store in Yuma in 1864. Removing some sacks from their pack horses, they entered the store and deposited $8,000 worth of gold. A few days later, after purchasing supplies, they mounted and rode out of town toward the east. There was considerable speculation as to who the men were, and more particularly, where they had secured the gold. Five Mexicans determined to find out. They trailed the Frenchmen east to Agua Caliente, where they found them camped at the hot springs almost on the Yuma-Maricopa County Line and directly south of the Eagle Tail Mountains.

The following day the three Frenchmen set out in a northerly direction, closely followed by the Mexicans. Suddenly the Frenchmen reversed their direction, confronted the Mexicans, and informed them that they knew they were being followed. The Frenchmen returned to Agua Caliente where they went through the motions of making a permanent camp. The ruse worked. During the night, the Frenchmen silently packed up and sneaked away while the Mexicans slept.

When the Mexicans missed the Frenchmen the next morning, they took up their trail and followed it into the Eagle Tail Mountains to a point where their tracks took off in three different directions. This was enough for the Mexicans. They returned to Yuma where they related their experience. The Frenchmen were never seen or heard of again, and their $8,000 deposit at Hooper's store was never claimed. It was assumed that they had met with a disaster of some kind.

In 1873, when King S. Woolsey, pioneer Indian fighter, was chasing a band of Apaches across western Arizona, his party passed through the Eagle Tail Mountains. Following a trail across Tenhachape Pass, they came upon a pile of rich gold ore which had obviously been placed there by parties unknown and with no attempt to conceal it. Some of the ore was taken to Yuma, where it was identifed as being exactly the same type as that traded by the three Frenchmen. The only explanation was that the Frenchmen, suddenly attacked by Indians, had dumped their gold ore to facilitate their escape. Had they not been chased down and killed, it was reasoned, they would have returned for the ore.

Yuma County—In the early 1900's, a stranger boarded an eastbound train at Needles, California, on the Colorado River. He struck up a conversation with the conductor and related that he was going to Illinois to get his son, who was going to return with him and help work a rich gold placer

94

he had found on the desert south of Topock. He showed the conductor a sack he said contained $30,000 worth of nuggets, and gave the railroader a handful.

Several months later the prospector was back in Needles, where he looked up the conductor and introduced his son. After outfitting themselves, the two left town.

After the passing of several weeks, the conductor became alarmed when they did not return and asked authorities to conduct a search for the missing men. When the posse returned with no news of the prospectors, the conductor hired two Indian trackers to search the area south of Topock. They returned and reported that the bodies of the father and son had been found beside their dead burros, all apparently killed by Indians. It is not known that this placer has ever been found.

Yuma County—Late in the year 1780, a Spanish expedition established the mission-pueblo of San Pedro y San Pablo de Bicuner on the California side of the Colorado River, a short distance below the present Laguna Dam at a site that is now bisected by the All-American Canal. Ruins of the mission-pueblo were uncovered during the construction of the canal, but nothing remains to indicate the site today.

On the California side of the Colorado River, and a short distance north of the mission-pueblo, were the famous Potholes gold placers which produced more than $2,000,000. Directly across the river on the Arizona side were the even richer Laguna placers, where the ground was so covered with gold that it could be picked up by the bucketfull. These two phenomenal placers were the traditional source of the Bicuner gold.

Employing the Yumas (Quechans) as forced laborers, the Spanish collected gold in unknown quantities on both sides of the Colorado. This wealth was taken to the mission-pueblo on the California side and stored. Tired of being subjugated by the Sapnish, the Indians arose in revolt in 1781, pillaged and burned the mission-pueblo, and killed or drove out the soldiers and padres. It is not known whether or not the Spanish had time to hide their accumulated gold before the sudden attack. If the Indians found the gold, their disposition of it is a matter of conjecture. Some believe the Indians dumped the gold into the Colorado River, while others say the gold was placed in rawhide bags, taken across the river to the Arizona side, and packed into the hills where it was concealed in a cave. This cave is sometimes placed on Sugarloaf Mountain, which is visible to the southeast from Laguna Dam.

Yuma County—John Gordon, a Scotsman, and Juan Perea, a Mexican, were a strange pair of prospecting partners as they worked their way up the Colorado Desert north of the Gila. Their luck had been miserable, and the heat was furnace-hot. They were out of food and desperately short of water.

But the Mexican was wise in the ways of the desert. "Look for a tinaja," he told his partner. "There we will find water." A tinaja (tank), the Mexican knew, was a natural bowl in the rocks that catches and holds water. They came to a huge boulder that offered some welcome shade, and settled down to contemplate their predicament. Certain death by dehydration was upon them. Suddenly the Mexican shouted, "Look!" His swollen eyes had settled upon the form of an animal approaching from the nearby hills. "It is a camel!" he cried.

Gordon could not believe his eyes, for indeed it was a camel. Neither men knew that it was a stray from Lt. Beale's experiment with camel transportation in the southwestern United States. Half delirious, the prospectors watched in amazement as the animal lumbered past them and disappeared behind the rock.

"He looks for water!" said the Mexican. "We will follow him!" They struggled to their feet and took out after the animal. It led them straight to a small tinaja. Not until sometime after the two men had quenched their thirst did they notice that the ground around the tank was literally covered with gold nuggets. They filled their pockets with what they could carry, replenished their canteens with water, and eventually made their way to Yuma. After they had recovered from their horrible experience, the two prospectors spent weeks in the Tank Mountains northeast of Yuma searching for the gold of the Camel's Tank. It was never found.

Yuma County—In 1699, Juan Mateo Manje accompanied Father Eusebio Kino on a journey from Mexico into what is now Arizona. They told the Indians they met that they were searching for a mysterious "Blue Mountain" which would be rich in silver ore. The Indians were familiar with the story because they had been told exactly the same thing by another Spanish expedition the previous year.

Not finding the Blue Mountain, the expedition turned south at the Gila River and skirted the eastern slopes of the Copper Mountains. Here they found slag tailings of ore from which gold had been extracted. Indians accompanying Kino's party denied any knowledge of the mine, although it was obvious from the type of metates scattered about that it had been Indians who had ground the ore.

Later Spanish expeditions in search of the mine from which the ore had been taken were unable to locate it, and it is belived that the Indians, now aware of the white man's greedy search for precious ores, obliterated every trace of it.

Yuma County—A "glory hole," in mining terminology, is an open pit or funnel-shaped excavation formed by drawing off soft or broken ore through an underground passage.

In 1909, fabulous Arizona humorist Dick Wick Hall grubstaked Shorty Alger and two men named Barker and Griffin to do some prospecting in the

Harcuvar Mountains northwest of Salome. Alger had worked the area years before and had picked up a very rich piece of ore, but he had not been able to locate its source.

The three men were climbing a small hill to the north of Tank Pass, short of water, provisions and temper. Alger slipped and stuck his pick into the ground to keep from falling. When he pulled it out, he found impaled on the point a gold nugget weighing more than a half pound. Three sacks of the ore picked up at the spot assayed in Phoenix at the incredible value of $338,510 to the ton!

When the news of the find got around, it touched off a stampede. Prospectors swarmed in from all parts of the country and staked out claims for miles around in all directions. Most of them found more rattlers and Gila monsters than gold, but the lucky ones found plenty of gold in the little basin atop the hill.

The original finders took out more than $100,000 from the "glory hole," and an unknown quantity was stolen by the hordes of boomers who rushed to the spot. All efforts to discover the downward trend of this freak have been fruitless and expensive, but many mining experts agree that there's more gold there.

Yuma County—Poncho was a Tonto Apache who lived on the San Carlos Indian Reservation in northeastern Arizona. Among his Mexican friends was a certain Jose Alvarado. When Pancho's small son became ill, the Alvarado family cared for him. When the boy was well again, Pancho wanted to show his thanks by telling Jose where there was a source of gold in the Little Horn Mountains of Yuma County. But, by the time he got around to it, the Alvarado family had already moved to a little town then known as Palomas, in Yuma County.

The Indian followed the Alvarados to Palomas and told Jose that he wanted to take him to a place where there was much gold. When the time came to go to the spot, Jose insisted in taking along some of his Mexican friends. The Indian reluctantly agreed. Trouble started almost immediately when some of the Mexicans refused to eat with the Apache. Jose and the other Mexicans announced their intentions of returning to Palomas. Pancho said he would stay in the area and do some hunting, but secretly he had made arrangements to meet Jose later at a certain waterhole.

On the appointed day, Jose appeared at the rendezvous, but soon he was joined by his Mexican friends who had followed him. In their absence, Pancho had recovered a large piece of gold-bearing ore from the site. Taking Jose aside, he showed it to him and gave him directions to the mine, but warned him to go alone. That night Pancho slipped out of camp and was never seen again.

Jose did not then search for the gold, nor did he tell the Mexicans that he knew where it was located. Shortly after his return to Palomas, he became seriously ill, but before his death he passed the secret location on to his young son. Years later the son searched for the landmarks described to him by his father, but was never able to find the spot.

Yuma County—In 1898 an unnamed Mexican was employed as a wood-cutter at the La Fortuna Mine southeast of Yuma. As he was returning to the Fortuna camp one night after a spree in Yuma, he became lost and exhausted his supply of water. Wandering off the main trail and into a side canyon a short distance north of the La Fortuna Mine, he discovered rich gold ore covering the side of a hill. Believing it was an outcropping of the Fortuna vein, which was pinching out at the time, he decided to keep his job as long as it lasted, and then secure the necessary backing and develop his find. However, upon returning to the Fortuna, he was immediately fired for being absent from his job.

With a reputation for boozing in Yuma, the Mexican failed to promote a grubstake, and he drifted about the country aimlessly from job to job. One day he showed up at the ranch of Juan Alvarado near Mohawk and asked for work. Alvarado felt pity for the aging man and gave him a job. Out of gratitude, and realizing that he would never mine the gold, the Mexican told his story to the rancher and offered to take him to it. Alvarado could not leave the ranch at the time, and he was skeptical of the Mexican's story. Eventually the worker was paid off and drifted away.

Years later, the woodcutter, now an old man and completely destitute, showed up at the Alvarado ranch again. This time he insisted that the rancher accompany him to the site of the gold strike. Convinced now that the Mexican was telling the truth, the two made a wide search of the area. When they abandoned the search, the Mexican disappeared and was never heard of again. Alvarado spent several years off and on in searching for the mine, but never found it.

Yuma County—In the early 1860's there was an adobe corral on the desert edge north of Yuma. It was located at the foot of a small hill that was covered with gravel and small black pebbles smoothly rounded by some ancient erosive action. Cowboys in the area found the rounded pebbles ideal for throwing at the cattle when they were being corraled.

There seems to be no record of who owned the ranch on which the corral stood, nor when it was built. It is stated, however, that the ranch was abandoned after an Indian raid in which some of the cowhands were killed and the cattle driven away.

One of the surviving cowboys from the ranch later drifted back east, still carrying in his pocket a couple of the rounded black pebbles. One day he happened to show them to a mining man who recognized them to be hematite. Breaking them open, he found them to be filled with free gold.

It was some years before the cowboy returned to Arizona to recover the gold. He located the ruins of the old corral, but a search of the hill above it failed to reveal a single black pebble. What had happened to them? Many who searched for them concluded that they had been washed away in a cloud-burst.

Yuma County—About 1855, two American prospectors returning east from the California gold fields camped at Tinajas Atlas along the old Camino del Diablo trail southeast of Yuma. On the following night they made camp at Tule Tank (not to be confused with Tule Well). In the morning one of the hobbled horses was missing. It was agreed between the two men that one would break camp and ride slowly on while the other went in search of the stray animal.

The horse was found feeding on the slope of a large hill nearby. As the rider was about to mount, he noted a large chunk of ore at his feet. It was rich in gold and similar rocks lay over a large area of the hillside. Gathering several pieces of the ore, the man rode off to overtake his partner.

In Sonoita, Mexico, the partners found their sample of ore to be full of gold—richer than anything they had seen in California. But they were without funds and short of provisions, and working the mine would be impossible until they raised a grubstake. A Mexican jabonero (soapmaker) heard of their plight and offered to advance the necessary funds in return for an interest in the mine.

Properly outfitted, the three men set out to relocate it. On the first night out they made camp at Agua Salada on the banks of the Rio Sonoita. Here they were attacked by Apaches and all three were left for dead. In a few hours, the jabonero regained consciousness, although he was badly wounded and partially blinded. Determining that his partners were dead, he finally made his way back to Sonoita where he told the story, exhibiting the samples of ore to prove it.

Yuma County—The Chemuhuevi Indians lived on both sides of the Colorado River around Yuma and to the north. One day their chief came into Yuma, then known as Arizona City, and offered a large chunk of gold in exchange for provisions and whiskey. Like most Indians, he had no real idea of the value of gold, nor did he care as long as it secured what he wanted at the moment.

The old chief's gold naturally created a lot of excitement and everyone wanted to know where it came from, but he was stolidly untalkative. He did get drunk, however, and taunted the white men with the statement that there was plenty, plenty of gold where this came from. They plied him with more whiskey. They made threats. But the chief's tongue never loosened.

Several times later the old chief came back to Yuma. Always he had more gold to trade, and always he ended up drunk, but he never talked. All attempts to follow him were a waste of time. He simply faded into the desert.

The chief's last remembered trip to Yuma was in 1863. Soon afterwards it was learned that he had been killed in a fight with his own people, who feared that his drinking sprees in Yuma would eventually lead to his telling the white men where the gold was secured.

As intensively as the Colorado River area north of Yuma has been prospected, it seems impossible that the Chemuhuevi chief's source of gold could have remained undiscovered to this day. But the desert winds in that region constantly scoop out and refill, scarcely leaving the surface of the earth unchanged from day to day. The gold could be there still.

ARIZONA

METAL DETECTOR SITES

The last listing under each county, where applicable, groups together the names of settlements or communities, the sites of which are believed to be located within the county and which have disappeared from maps since 1886, from census records since 1885, and from early post office records. Where known, the 1885 population of these "vanished" towns is given (in brackets), together with any clues as to their possible locations. Facts pertaining to these possible ghost towns are generally too vague to justify individual listings.

It is emphasized that these are *possible* ghost towns, and that, in some instances, they may not be ghosts at all, but surviving today under names different than their originals. Many early community names were changed as a matter of pride, the once popular suffix of "ville," "burg" and "borough" being dropped as communities grew larger in size. Others had their names changed because their originals were· just not satisfactory to later generations of inhabitants.. And some were forced to change their names by post office officials to eliminate confusing duplications.

Many of the pioneer communities in Arizona consisted of nothing more than a few crude houses—even tents—clustered around a mill in a mining area. As ores were depleted, most of these towns vanished, some completely lost today. Possibly the sites of some of these forgotten. towns have never been searched for relics, and are thus virgin fields for metal detectors. How to locate the sites of these completely forgotten ghost towns becomes the problem! In our opinion, this can best be accomplished through your own research in county seats. From their formation, almost all counties had some kind of organization and maintained some kind of records. It is in these early records that clues to the locations of vanished towns will most likely be located. Where these records have been preserved, and are made available to you, it is our belief that through some diligent research, your chance of coming up with the site of a genuine and unexplored ghost town are excellent.

Apache County—On the night of October 30, 1947, a meteorite disintegrated 15 to 20 miles high above a point estimated to have been about halfway between Rock Point, Arizona (State 63), and Shiprock, New Mexico. Scientists estimate that fragments were scattered over an area 20 to 30 miles in length in all directions. In searching for fragments of this meteorite, remember that they may or may not be valuable, depending upon whether it is the stony type (95 percent are, and they are of little value) or the nickle-iron type, which are of some value.

Most searchers for meteorite fragments look for a crater, but scientists point out that a meteorite disintegrating in the atmosphere at this height makes no crater. Scientists also say that one can never tell what a meteorite specimen is going to look like. The best bet is to look for a grey, granular stone covered with a black fusion crust. But sometimes meteorite fragments are black inside and out, and a few are almost white.

Although this meteorite is a matter of scientific record, not one fragment of it is known to have been found. If you find a fragment you think might be from this meteorite, take it or send it to the American Meteorite Museum, Winslow, Arizona. Tell them exactly where you found it. They will tell you whether or not you have found anythin gof value.

Apache County—Inquire in Chambers (US 66) for directions to the Kin Tiel Navajo ruins, about 18 miles away. Covering almost 30 acres, this is among the larger pueblo sites in the Southwest. Most of the walls have been razed and the site was excavated in 1929.

Apache County—Inquire in the town of Navajo (Interstate 40) for directions to Navajo Springs, about four miles away. It was here that the territorial government was set up in 1863, but nothing remains at the site.

Apache County—Inquire in Lupton (Interstate 40) for directions to ancient ruins in the vicinity of Battleship Mountain. Some archaeologists believe that these are the ruins of one of the Seven Cities of Cibola described by Friar Marcos de Niza who accompanied the Coronado expedition in 1540. There are other widely scattered ruins in the area, and little excavating has been done. The sites are all located on the Navajo reservation and permission to explore must be secured from the tribal council as well as the Federal government.

Apache County—Other possible ghost towns include Aqua, at the head of Lithodonron Wash in an area where there are only trails. This is located on the Navajo Indian Reservation; Billings (20), once a station on the Southern Pacific Railroad near the point where US 66 enters Petrified Forest National Park; Brigham City (190); Bush Valley (50), west of St. Johns and probably near the town of Concho; Los Gigantes, near Los Gigantes Buttes in the western stretches of Lukachukai Mountains. On the Navajo Indian Reservations; Nero, on the west bank of the Little Colorado River south of St. Johns; Ojo Puerte, on the west bank of Chinle Wash, south of the Red

ARIZONA

Rock Trading Post on the Navajo Indian Reservation; Pueblo Colorado; Salado Spring, on the east side of the Little Colorado River, south of St. Johns; Viborad, near the head of Lithodondron Wash. On Navajo Indian Reservation; Washington Pass; White Rock Spring, on Pueblo Colorado Wash northwest of Cross Canyon Trading Post, on the Navajo Indian Reservation.

Cochise County—Inquire in Dragoon (Interstate 10) for directions to the ghost town of Middlemarch. Once a copper camp of about 100 population, nothing remains today except assorted ruins.

Cochise County—Ask in Tombstone (US 80) for directions to the ghost town of Millville, located on the east bank of the San Pedro River directly opposite the site of Charleston (see below). Actually the two were one town, and both were essentially abandoned when water flooded the nearby Tombstone mines. Only the remains of a few mill buildings mark the site.

Cochise County—Inquire in Tombstone (US 80) for directions to the ghost town of Charleston, on the west bank of the San Pedro River eight miles to the southwest. The site is marked by a cluster of tall cottonwood trees and scattered crumbling walls. It is comparatively easy of access and thus attracts a lot of visitors. World War II soldiers from Fort Huachuca held exercises here and their bazooka shells and several earthquakes have added to the wreckage.
Charleston was founded in the late 1870's as the mill town for the Tombstone mines because the latter lacked the necessary water. It started downhill about 1900, and by 1921 its population had moved away. The town had no government, no city hall, no jail—only a justice of the peace who needed no jail because he killed his men. It was one of the wildest towns in Arizona, the hangout of outlaws of all descriptions. This once booming community is rapidly falling into complete decay, and no one seems to care.

Cochise County— The marked site of Fort Crittenden is on State 82 about three miles south of the town of Sonoita. It lies within the boundaries of Coronado National Forest. Formerly called Fort Buchanan (at a site a mile away), it was used as a storehouse for large quantities of military supplies, said to have been valued at $1,000,000 at one time. At the outbreak of the Civil War these were destroyed on the spot to prevent the possibility of their falling into Confederate hands. Its numerous adobe structures are rapidly disappearing. A ruined wall or two are all that mark the site of nearby Fort Buchanan.

Cochise County—Inquire in Huachuca City (State 90) for directions to the ghost town of Sunnyside, in the Huachuca Mountains. Founded in

1890 as a religious colony, the community had a peak population of only 50, sharing their work, income and food in communal style. The people of Sunnyside were known as Donnellites, or Copper Glance Christians after the Copper Glance Mine that was operated to support the community. The town became a ghost about 1930 when the ore ran out and copper prices declined. Most of the town's old buildings have collapsed.

Cochise County—Inquire in Willcox (Interstate 10) for directions to Dos Cabezas, a rapidly crumbling ghost town that has been described as the oldest surviving ghost town in Arizona. In the surrounding hills and mountains are active gold and silver mines, originally worked by prospectors who relied upon the soldiers of Fort Bowie for protection against the Apaches. Long before the Spanish arrived in Cochise County, Dos Cabezas was an Apache encampment clustered around what later became known as Elwell Spring. This became an important stop on the Butterfield Overland Mail route until the government ordered the route changed at the outbreak of the Civil War. Built in 1858, the old stage station, scene of many Apache attacks, is still standing in an advanced stage of decay.

By 1876 Dos Cabezas boasted of having 42 school age children, but the town did not hit its peak population until 1909, when copper was discovered nearby and mines developed by the Mascot Copper Company. On the desert near Dos Cabezas, the company built a town called Mascot, now also a ghost. The boom at Dos Cabezas was headlined across the United States, and lasted for 20 years. With the depression of 1929, however, the copper company pulled out, dismantled Mascot, and nearby Dos Cabezas became a ghost, the better buildings being sold and demolished for their lumber. Only a few old adobe structures still endure, and the few people who live here today are surrounded with crumbling walls and piles of debris.

Cochise County—A few people still live in Pearce, on US 666 about 29 mines south of Willcox, but it is essentially a ghost town. John Pearce, a rancher, made a gold strike here in 1894. The community that grew up around the mine rapidly became a fair-sized city. The peak of production was reached in 1896, but the mine was operated until 1904 when a cave-in caused it to shut down. In the late 1890's, besides its mining activity, Pearce became a rip-roaring cowboy town, and was headquarters of the Alvord-Stiles gang. To frustrate outlaws, gold bullion in the form of bars too heavy to be carried out on horseback were transported to the Cochise station in ordinary farm wagons.

By 1919 Pearce had a population of 1,500, a school, restaurants, boarding houses, saloons, hotels, motion picture theater and other businesses. People began drifting away in the 1930's, and today only a store or two remain.

ARIZONA

Cochise County—Inquire in Bowie (Interstate 10) for directions to the ruins of Fort Bowie. Established in 1862 at the eastern entrance to Apache Pass, it was considered the most dangerous point on the emigrant road to California. The pass became the grave of many soldiers, prospectors and Travelers. Stagecoach drivers who had to go through the pass from 1861 to 1874, when the Apaches were on the warpath, were offered triple their ordinary pay. Few lived to collect it. Thick adobe walls mark the site of the fort located on the summit of of a flat-topped hill. Remnants of about 30 other buildings are scattered over a five-acre tract among mesquite, greasewood and scrub brush.

Cochise County—Inquire in Cochise (US 666) for directions to Sulphur Spring in Sulphur Spring Valley east of Dragoon. Here was the only water available to emigrant trains between Apache Pass and Dragoon Springs. Many wagon trains made camp here and the threat of an Indian attack was always imminent.

Cochise County—Inquire in Tombstone (US 80) for directions to the near ghost town of Paradise, located on East Turkey Creek about one mile south of the site of the ghost town of Galeyville. Paradise was established after the discovery of copper in the Chiricahua Mountains, and the town's reputation for lawlessness soon rivaled that of Tombstone and Galeyville. At one time the town had more than 100 houses and business establishments. The end of prosperity came to Paradise with the panic of 1907 when the bottom dropped out of copper prices. Merchants closed their doors and families moved away. A few people hung on, and a few moved back in recent years, but Paradise is essentially a ghost of the past.

Cochise County—The ghost town of Galeyville, one of the most famous in Arizona, is located in a small, well-watered canyon in the Chiricahua Mountains. When mining became unprofitable in the region, Galeyville became a resort for American and Mexican rustlers and smugglers, with some of America's most famous outlaws making it their headquarters. Free from any law, Galeyville prospered until Sheriff John Slaughter, disturbed by the stealing of his own cattle, cleaned the outlaws from the area.
In 1881 Galeyville had 11 saloons, six or more stores, two hotels, restaurants, butcher shops, lumber yards and many other establishments. As the Phoenix *Herald* pointed out at the time, the town had everything but a jail, a church and a school. Nothing at all remains of Galeyville today.

Cochise County—Inquire in Bernardino (US 80) for directions to San Bernardino, almost on the Mexican border to the south. This was once the headquarters of the San Bernardino Ranch, an early Spanish hacienda and army post. John Slaughter purchased the ranch in 1884 and began his slow

TREASURE GUIDE

campaign to clean the surrounding country of outlaws. **Map Code 8 G-6**

Cochise County—The town of Fairbank, on State 82 west of Tombstone, is hardly a ghost, but its buildings are half empty. Fairbank is a far cry from the turbulent 1880's when it was a busy supply point for Tombstone and served the many freighters hauling ore from the Tombstone mines to the mills at Contention City and Charleston. It was an important point on the railroad between Guaymas, Mexico and Benson, Arizona, and a stage station for mail and express. There was an Indian village called Santa Cruz on this site in 1700, and after heavy rains, bones, ollas, arrowheads and pieces of broken pottery are found.

Cochise County—Inquire in Fairbank (State 82) for directions to the ruins of Quibiri, a mission founded by Father Eusebio Kino sometime before 1700. It was on a direct line between San Xavier and the Apache stronghold in the Dragoon Mountains, and it saw a great deal of fighting. The structure was in the nature of a fort with four walls each about 300 feet in length, with the only entrance on the east facing the San Pedro River. The walls are remarkably well preserved.

Cochise County—About 14 miles south of Fairbank, at a point on State 82 in the Whetstone Mountains where Granite Peak can be seen to the west, is the scene of a skirmish fought in 1871 between Apaches and soldiers pursuing Chief Cochise. Many artifacts have been found in the area.

Cochise County—Inquire in Tombstone (US 80) for directions to Courtland, a near ghost town located on an unimproved road about 19 miles to the northeast. It was founded in 1909 by a miner in an area where copper and some gold are still mined. With a population of 2,000, the town had many businesses, including two stage stations, two newspapers, and a motion picture theater. Only the skeletons of a few buildings remain today.

Cochise County—The remains of Contention City are located on the east bank of the San Pedro River west of Tombstone. This was the site of the stamp mills for crushing the ore brought here from the Tombstone mines. Although the town had a life of no longer than 10 years, it supported a number of stores, saloons and boarding houses. When the Tombstone mines closed because of flooding, the Contention City mills closed and the town died. Only a few crumbling adobes and traces of a small cemetery mark the site.

Cochise County—Inquire in Tombstone (US 80) for directions to the site of Gleeson, about 16 miles to the east. Before the Spaniards arrived

106

in Arizona, turquoise was mined here by the Indians. When copper, lead and silver was discovered in the area, Gleeson boomed. Almost destroyed by a fire in 1912, the town rebuilt, but by 1940 it lost its post office and most of its people moved away. Today there are a few residents, but most of the old town is in ruins. Nearby is the site of an old mining camp called Turquoise. Nothing at all remains of it.

Cochise County—Inquire in Sierra Vista (State 90) for directions to the site of Garces, a now completely vanished mining camp located about 10 miles to the south and close to the Mexican border. It once had several stores and a population of about 200.

Cochise County—Inquire in Sierra Vista (State 90) for directions to the site of Hamburg, about 15 miles to the south. Once a mining camp of about 150 people, the town, located in Ramsey Canyon, had several stores and dwellings. Absolutely nothing but the site exists today.

Cochise County—Ask in San Simon (Interstate 10) for directions to the site of Hilltop, an old mining camp. Originally located on Shaw Peak, the town was later moved to another nearby site. At one time it had a population of about 100 and had the usual mining camp assortment of buildings, all of which are in ruins today.

Cochise County—Inquire in Benson (Interstate 10) for directions to the remains of Johnson, once an important copper mining camp of some 1,000 people. Scattered concrete foundations and wrecked mill buildings remain to indicate the site.

Cochise County—Ask in Willcox (Interstate 10) for directions to the abandoned town of Russellville, about 16 miles southeast. A mining camp of about 100 population and with several commercial buildings at its peak, the town moved to Johnson when it was founded nearer the Peabody Mine. Only the wrecks of a few buildings remain today.

Cochise County—Other possible ghost towns include Cochise Spring, on the northern fringes of the Dragoon Mountains; Drew's Station (25); Ochoville (50), on the Southern Pacific Railroad near the Mexican border; Sand Springs, in the Perilla Mountains south of the town of Perilla and almost on the Mexican border; Steele's Station, northwest of Willcox; Teviston (100), on the Southern Pacific Railroad near Bowie; Tres Alamos, on the San Pedro River in the northwestern section of the county; Vota, west of the San Pedro River in the southwestern corner of the county.

Coconino County—Inquire at Marble Canyon Lodge (Alternate US 89) for directions to the site of Lee's Ferry, on the Colorado River at the mouth of

Paria Creek. It is a drive of about six miles over an unimproved road that is often little more than a dry creek bed. From 1872 to the completion of the Navajo Bridge in 1912, it was the only crossing of the Colorado for a distance of 100 miles. It was established by John D. Lee, a Mormon pioneer who, with his family, settled here, built a log cabin, and acquired the ferry rights at a point held by the Mormon Church. After Lee's execution for his part in the infamous Mountain Meadows Massacre, his widow operated the ferry and finally sold it to the Mormon Church. The Lee log cabin and a few outbuildings still stand.

Coconino County—Inquire in Winona (just off Interstate 10 east of Flagstaff) for directions to the preserved remains of Pit House of the early Pueblo period. Only the walls still stand. This is one of the largest of the pit houses found in the Southwest. It was excavated in 1936, but many artifacts are still found in the surrounding area.

Coconino County—Inquire in Flagstaff (Interstate 17-40) for directions to the Turkey Hill ruins, pueblo-like structures built between 1203 and 1278 A.D.

Coconino County—Inquire in Sedona (Alternate US 89) for directions to the Red Rocks, ancient dwellings built in man-made caves. Many artifacts have been found in this region.

Coconino County—Possible ghost towns include Camp Lincoln, believed to have been located in the general vicinity of Sedona; Hatche's Wells, on Moencopi Wash west of the town of Moencopi (State 264) and near the Navajo County line; Pamela, probably an old station on the Santa Fe Railroad in the vicinity of Williams; Snyder's Hole, probably at the head of Oak Creek Canyon south of Flagstaff; Thousand Wells, in the area east of Tonalea (State 64) and probably near the Navajo County line; Waterpocket, probably in the area of Moencopi; Willow Springs (still shown on some maps), just to the east of US 89 at the junction of a dirt road cutting east to Tuba City.

Gila County—Inquire in Globe (US 60) for directions to the ghost town of McMillenville. Only a few adobe ruins, a broken-down stamp mill, and the great Stonewall Jackson shaft mark the site of this once important mining town. Charles McMillen and his tenderfoot partner, Theodore "Dory" Harris, accidentally discovered silver here in 1876 while Harris slept off a drunk and McMillen poked around nearby. Around the Stonewall Jackson Mine a camp of 1,700 people sprang up almost overnight. After Harris and McMillen took out $60,000 in ore they sold their mine for $160,000. The new owner took out $2,000,000. McMillen drank himself to death within a few months, and Harris lost his entire fortune on the San Francisco Mining Exchange in less than 90 days. He ended up washing dishes in a Globe restaurant.

Gila County—In the vicinity of Peridot, an Indian community on US 70, are found many rough peridots and smoky topaz stones which make beautiful necklaces and rings. The site is on the San Carlos Indian Reservation.

Gila County—The town of Inspiration is just to the north of US 60 between Globe and Miami. Inquire here for directions to the remains of the Mexican village of Los Adobes, which was abandoned when the land around it began to sink.

Gila County—Inquire in Miami (US 60) for directions to Bloody Tanks, the site of an engagement in 1864 between a party of whites and their Maricopa Indian allies on one side, and Apaches, who greatly outnumbered them, on the other. Because of their superior arms and clever strategy, the Americans under the command of King S. Woolsey lost only one man. Many relics of the fight have been found in the area.

Gila County—Inquire in Miami (US 60) for directions to the Pinal Ranch, once known as the Irons Ranch, about seven miles away. In early times the site was occupied by a band of Apaches. It is in an almost impregnable fastness surrounded by lookout peaks and accessible only by obscure trails. In 1870, Camp Pinal, garrisoned with 400 cavalrymen, was located here.

Gila County—Inquire in Young (State 288) for directions to the site of the Battle of Big Dry Wash between Indians from the San Carlos Indian Reservation and troops of the Sixth and Third Cavalry. Only a few Indians escaped the attack, leaving relics scattered over a wide area.

Gila County—Inquire in Young (State 288) for directions to the following sites which figured in the famous Graham-Tewksbury feud: The site of the elder Tewksbury ranch, on the Cherry Creek Road, is marked only by the remnants of a chimney. The site of the Stinson ranch on the Young-Holbrook Road was for years a noted landmark, but nothing remains of it today. The old Graham cabin still stands on the Young ranch. During the feud days, it was the stronghold of the Graham faction. It is now sagging and rapidly disappearing.

Gila County—Inquire in Young (State 288) for directions to the Indian Cliff Dwellings at the head of Cherry Creek. Built between 1348 and 1385 by a branch of the Zuni, they have suffered little from vandalism because of their inaccessibility.

TREASURE GUIDE

Gila County—Inquire in Claypool (US 60) for directions to Burch, still a small copper mining camp on the banks of Pinal Creek, but nothing compared to its size at the height of the silver stampede that began here in 1876 when numerous small silver and gold mines opened on Sleeping Beauty Mountain and in the hills to the west. Most of these are now covered with tailing dumps. Much of the ore in these mines was near the surface and quickly played out.

Gila County—Inquire in Globe (US 60-70) for directions to Wheatfields, a small settlement that was once an Apache agricultural community on the Apache Trail. It was at one time the site of a silver mill, and in 1864 whites raided the spot and destroyed the Indian crops. Before the Globe bonanza was discovered, Wheatfields was visited by many prospectors seeking the rich mines that were reported to exist in the area. In the vicinity are said to be located at least three lost mines.

Gila County—The entire breathtaking 79 miles of State 88 from Claypool to Apache Junction is known as Apache Trail. Just to the east of the road, about 13 miles north of Claypool, is a rugged mountain known as Smoke Signal Peak, one of several in the vicinity once used by Indians for communicating by smoke signals. Smoke Signal Peak was also used by Federal troops as a station for heliograph and wigwag signals. To the east of the road, about 18 mines north of Claypool, can be seen the rugged Sierra Anchas where there are the ruins of several prehistoric dwellings, some of which are known only to cowboys who have discovered them in precipitous canyons far from beaten paths. Many artifacts have been found in this area which one should not enter without the aid of a competent guide.

Gila County—The little town of Christmas, on State 77 about nine miles north of Winkelman, was once an important mining center, but more recently was famous for the heavy volume of mail handled at Christmas time. Although a hundred or more people still live here, there is no longer a post office and the town is a combination of old and new buildings, some of the latter falling into decay.

Gila County—Inquire in Seneca (US 60) for directions to the near ghost town of Chrysotile, an asbestos mining camp at the bottom of Ash Creek Canyon, which is more than 1,000 feet deep and 4,000 feet wide at this point. A few people still live here, but most of the town's original buildings are gone or rapidly disappearing.

Gila County—Inquire in Hayden (State 177) for directions to the site of Chilito, once a copper mining camp with a peak population of about 200. The town declined about 1921 and what buildings remain standing are now

ARIZONA

used by ranchers.

Gila County—Inquire in Globe (US 60-70) for directions to what is
left of the ghost town of Copper Hill, about four miles northwest. This important but short-lived camp once had several stores, offices, boarding houses,
a school and a hospital, but all that marks the site today are a few cement
foundations, mine dumps and scattered ruins.

Gila County—Inquire in Globe (US 60-70) for directions to the site of
Nugget, once a silver mining camp of about 100 population at its peak.
Nothing at all remains today of the few houses, stores, post office and saloon
the town once boasted.

Gila County—Inquire in Globe (US 60-70) for directions to the site
of Pioneer, once a lively silver mining camp with a school, brewery, bank, saw-
mill, several stores and a hotel. Located on the slopes of Pioneer Mountain,
the town once had a population of about 350. Nothing is visible today except
some old foundations.

Gila County—Inquire in Miami (US 60) for directions to the remains
of Bellevue, about five miles to the southwest. All that remains of this old
copper camp that once had a population of about 300 are some scattered
foundations and ruined buildings. The town had a stage station, a few general
stores, a boarding house, livery stable and post office.

Gila County—Possible ghost towns include Armer; Catalpa; Little Giant;
probably in the area of El Capitan Mountain in the southeastern corner of
the county; Reno (200), on Clear Creek in the extreme northwestern corner of
the county; Salt River (35); Tonto (100).

Graham County—Inquire in Solomon (US 70) for directions to a prehistoric ruin believed to be the Chichilticalli (the Red House) mentioned by
several early Spanish explorers including Coronado. Only a reddish colored
mound remains.

Graham County—Inquire in Thatcher (US 70) for directions to Red
Knolls, a natural rock amphitheater. Foundations of common pit houses, bits
of broken pottery, arrowheads, and manos and metates are still to be found.
It is believed that these heights were prized as a lookout and signaling point
during the Indian warfare years. The two old military posts of Camp Godwin
and Camp Thomas are visible from here to the northwest. Rustlers used
the coves and bays of the knolls as corrals for holding and branding stolen
cattle.

Graham County—Possible ghost towns include Dunlap (300); Eureka

111

TREASURE GUIDE

Spring, on Aravapai Creek in the southwestern corner of the county; Green's Camp, in the northern tip of the Gila Mountains on the San Carlos Indian Reservation; Mingville, in the southwestern section of the county, probably in the northern reaches of the Galiuro Mountains; Purdy (200); Layton (20); Reiley Wells, near Reiley Hill in the southwestern corner of the county. The latter also appeared on old maps as Riley and Rilay.

Greenlee County—Inquire in Clifton (US 666) for directions to the site of the ghost town of Metcalf, about seven miles distant, and tucked between the granite cliffs of Chase Creek Canyon. Settled in 1872 when gold was discovered here, it boomed to a population of about 5,000. Some of the richest mineral deposits were found in Gold Gulch about a mile north of the site. Frequent outlaw and Indian raids troubled the town's beginning, and when the gold and copper played out, the town died. Among the ruined buildings here, now practically reduced to rubble, are a bank, school, hospital, dairy, movie theater, several stores and dwellings.

Maricopa County—Inquire in Tortilla Flat (State 88) for directions to Horse Mesa Dam on the Salt River. The gorge near the dam is extremely narrow. Two-thirds up the face of the rocky wall on the road side of the river is a ledge with a natural cave. A guide is absolutely essential to reach this cave, which the Apaches considered one of their safest and strongest retreats. This was the scene of the Battle of the Caves in 1872, between Federal troops and Indians.

Maricopa County—Inquire in Gila Bend (Interstate 8) for directions to an early Indian fortress in the Gila Bend Mountains. Old trails lead throughout the village which consisted of some 40 houses. Many artifacts have been recovered in the area.

Maricopa County—Inquire in Wickenburg (US 60-89-93) for directions to the site of Seymour, once a mill town for the famous Vulture Mine about 10 miles distant. The camp had only a single main street, but more than a score of buildings and a population of 300. When the mill was moved to the mine, the people of Seymour packed up and moved away. Nothing remains today but ruins and rubble.

Maricopa County—Inquire in Wickenburg (US 60-89-93) for directions to Vulture City, the mining community for the famed Vulture Mine discovered by Henry Wickenburg. The town probably had a peak population of 100. Of the town's several buildings, the Old Rock House and the mill are still standing. Wells Fargo chests, carrying gold from the mine on stages, were so often seized by bandits that the lives of bullion carriers were always in jeopardy. Some of these chests were rifled in the area. It is believed that others were probably abandond and that treasure could still exist in the

ARIZONA

vicinity. Map Code 8 D-3

Maricopa County—Inquire in Wickenburg (US 60-89-93) for directions to Culling's Well, about six miles west. The place was named for Tom Culling, an Englishman who established a station here on the old stage road. When Joe Drew took the station over in the 1860's, he kept a lantern burning at night on a high pole for the guidance of desert travelers.

Maricopa County—Possible ghost towns include Kennedy's Station, on the south bank of the Gila River west of Gila Bend; Moore's Station (25); Overton, southeast of Rock Springs; Maryville, on the north bank of the Gila River just west of its junction with the Verde River; Painted Rock, on the Southern Pacific Railroad east of Sentinel; Saucita; Smith's Mill, on the east bank of the Hassayampa River southeast of Wickenburg; Zenos.

Mohave County—Inquire in Kingman (US 66) for directions to the site of Golconda, about 15 miles to the north. Only one or two buildings, some old foundations and a pile of mill tailings mark the site. The town was virtually destroyed by a fire in 1917 and died completely with a decline in the price of lead and zinc.

Mohave County—Inquire in Kingman (US 66) for directions to the site of Frisco, an old mining town virtually located over a gold deposit. With a peak population of about 150, Frisco was unique among mining towns for its quiet and peaceful nature. Nothing remains but the site.

Mohave County—Inquire in Kingman (US 66) for directions to the ghost town of White Hills. The town was originally known as "Indian Secret Mining District," so named because Indians knew of the presence of minerals here but kept the information from white men. When an Indian gave the secret to Henry Shaffer in 1892, many silver mines sprang up in the area and the town of White Hills was born, soon booming to a population of 2,000. Today it is nothing but a group of crumbling ruins.

Mohave County—Inquire in Kingman (US 66) for directions to the site of Katherine, about five miles northeast of Davis Dam on the Colorado River. The camp boomed in the mid-1920's as gold mining activity increased in the area, but died in the 1930's. Hardly anything is left today except the ruins of Katherine Mine.

Mohave County—Inquire in Kingman (US 66) for directions to the site of Stockton, once one of the most active mining camps in Mohave County. Located about eight miles north of Kingman, a few abandoned buildings are

113

all that remain to indicate the site. Map Code 8 B-2

Mohave County—Inquire in Kingman (US 66) for directions to the site of Goldflat, once a small mining community located about three miles southwest. Never very large, the mines supporting the camp produced $7,000,000 worth of gold. The town is in complete ruins.

Mohave County—Inquire in Kingman or Topock (both on US 66) for directions to Oatman, about 30 miles from either place. Although Oatman still appears on modern maps, it is now a ghost town that strings up and down the foothills of the Black Mountains. Throughout its entire history, Oatman alternately prospered and languished after the fashion of many mining towns. In the early days of the camp a narrow gauge railroad ran from the mines nearby to Fort Mohave on the Colorado River, and to this point a ferry brought supplies from Needles, California. From 1904 to 1907, $3,000,000 worth of ore was taken from the mines in this vicinity, and the town boasted two banks, 10 stores, several saloons and other business establishments. The town almost died with the decline in mining activity, and the relocation of US 66 spelled its doom. Several abandoned buildings still stand.

Mohave County—The small settlement of Yucca (US 66) between Kingman and Topock is a ghost of the past. The town formerly catered to employees of the nearby Yucca-Tungsten, Borrianna, and Signal Mines. When the production of ores declined, the town all but died.

Mohave County—Inquire in Kingman (US 66) for directions to the ghost town of Goldroad, located just north of the ghost town of Oatman. The town once had about 400 wooden stores and tent dwellings, but died with the decline of Oatman. Nothing at all remains but the ruins of a few homes, mine shafts, heads, mills and dumps. Gila monsters and rattlesnakes are plentiful here among the thorny ocotillos and chollas.

Mohave County—Inquire in Kingman (US 66) for directions to the site of Cerbat, about 12 miles to the northwest. Once the seat of Mohave County, the town had several stores, saloons, a courthouse, city hall and a smelter during its boom years. Only the ruins of the mill and some stone walls still stand to mark the site of this once most important silver and lead mining camp in the Hualapai district.

Mohave County—Inquire in Kingman (US 66) for directions to the site of the ghost town of Mineral Park, once the seat of Mohave County. The center of a rich and extensive silver mining area, the camp was once the largest town in the county, supporting several saloons and gambling halls, stores, a five-stamp mill, a school, newspaper, hotel and four restaurants.

The town attained a population of about 700 at its peak, having a large Chinese section and red light district. When a decline in mining activities set in about 1885, the county seat was moved to Kingman, spelling the death of Mineral Park. A few modern mining operations are conducted in the area, but about all that remains of Mineral Park are adobe and rock ruins.

Mohave County—Inquire in Kingman (US 66) for directions to the site of the ghost town of Oldtrails, located about one mile south of the ghost town of Oatman. The town was founded in 1915 to be nearer some of the important mines than Oatman, and flourished until about 1925 when mining declined in the region. With a peak population of about 500, Oldtrails had every modern convenience of its day including telegraph and telephone service and electricity. It boasted a fine hospital, numerous stores, sheet metal works, a bottling plant and other establishments. Of all these buildings, only one or two remain today.

Mohave County—The site of Aubrey Landing, or Aubrey City, is located two miles northeast of Parker Dam on the Colorado River. It became the distributing center for supplies to the mines and camps of the Bill Williams Basin. By 1886 the post office closed because the town was almost dead. Most, if not all, of the site is today under the waters of Havasu Lake.

Mohave County—Inquire in Wikieup (US 93) for directions to the ghost town of Signal, about 22 miles to the southeast. Springing into life almost overnight as the mill town for a group of important mines, Signal grew into a town of several hundred people and some 200 buildings. Eventually the mines, reduced in activity, could not support the town and by 1932 Signal was all but deserted.

Mohave County—Inquire in Wikieup (US 93) for directions to the site of Owens, an old lead and silver mining camp located at the base of McCracken Hill about four miles to the south. Founded in the 1870's, the town never reached more than 150 population.

Mohave County—Inquire in Wikieup (US 93) for directions to the site of Greenwood City, once a thriving town of some 400 population. The camp was supported by mills treating the ore from nearby mines. In the late 1870's the erection of a larger and newer mill at nearby Virginia City (now also a ghost) spelled Greenwood City's doom. Little remains today except the site.

Mohave County—Inquire in Wikieup (US 93) for directions to the site of Cedar, about 15 miles northwest. Located on the east slope of the Hualapai Mountains, the camp was the trading center for the gold, silver and copper mines in the area. Its peak population reached about 200, but nothing is visible of the town today except some scattered rock ruins and foundations.

Mohave County—Inquire in Wikieup (US 93) for directions to the site of Alamo Crossing, on the north bank of the Bill Williams River about 30 miles to the south. This small mining community was supported largely by a 50-stamp mill, but when the supply of ore diminished, the camp was abandoned. Nothing stands today and the site is probably difficult to reach.

Mohave County—Inquire in Wikieup (US 93) for directions to the site of American Flag, in the Hualapai Mountains about 25 miles to the northwest. The place was all but abandoned when mining activities ceased about 1890. Very little remains to mark the site, and it should not be confused with another camp of the same name in Pinal County.

Mohave County—Inquire in Wikieup (US 93) for directions to the site of Virginia City, once an important mill town located about 22 miles to the south and directly across an arroyo from the mining camp of Signal. Virginia City's peak population was about 700. Only the ruins of the mill are still visible.

Mohave County—Only a few building foundations remain to mark the site of Germa, located about two miles southwest of the ghost town of Oatman. The camp died about 1906.

Mohave County—Polhamus Landing was a Colorado River port at approximately where Davis Dam now stands. It consisted of a large warehouse and a few other scattered buildings. When railroads built into the area, the town died.

Mohave County—Hardyville was established in 1864 when Capt. William H. Hardy began operating a ferry, trading post and inn on the Colorado River about two miles south of the present town of Bullhead City. Once the seat of Mohave County, the town boomed, but it was struck by two disastrous fires and then died when the railroad was built across the Colorado River at Needles. The buildings of the old town have completely vanished with only the old cemetery still visible.

Mohave County—Inquire in Peach Springs (US 66) for directions to Diamond Canyon. This was once a popular place from which to view Grand Canyon. Diamond Creek Hotel stood here until the railroad between Williams and Grand Canyon was built in 1907. The hotel was a frame structure with nine bedrooms, a dining room and lobby. After its abandonment, it was carried off piecemeal by ranchers and Indians until only the foundations remain today.

Mohave County—Gold Basin may still be found on some maps, but it is virtually a ghost town, located to the north of Kingman about 50 miles. Although there were productive mines in the area, Gold Basin never achieved any appreciable size, and what there was of it has all but disappeared today.

Mohave County—Located on the Colorado River about one-half mile north of old Fort Mojave, Mohave City was not so much a river port as it was a trading and recreational center for the California Volunteers stationed at the fort. Selected as the first seat of Mohave County, the town flourished until the boundaries of Fort Mohave were expanded to include the town. Residents were ordered to evacuate the area within 30 days. When the military moved in they tore down the buildings they could not occupy. Today only cellar depressions mark the site, and these are located on the Mojave Indian Reservation.

Mohave County—The ghost town of Lost Basin will be difficult to locate. It was situated eight miles south of the old Scanlon Ferry crossing of the Colorado River and about 65 miles north of Kingman (US 66), where inquiries should be made. Nothing remains to mark the site.

Mohave County—The near ghost town of Chloride is located at the terminus of State 62, four miles east of US 93 at a point 19 miles north of Kingman. While its glory lasted little more than a year, Chloride had at its peak a population of about 1,500, a newspaper, 13 saloons, and numerous stores and shops. Today a hundred or so people still live here amid the ruins of a mill and mines.

Mohave County—Hackberry still appears on some maps, but it is virtually a ghost town, located on US 66 about 30 miles northeast of Kingman. Contending for the county seat with Kingman in 1866, Hackberry came in second. After the mines declined, Hackberry all but died.

Mohave County—The site of Liverpool Landing, once called Pittsburg Landing, is on the Colorado River about 20 miles north of Parker Dam. It served as the supply point for the Owens mining district, and collapsed with the decline of mining activities in the region. Possibly the site is under the waters of Havasu Lake.

Mohave County—Possible ghost towns include Altoohah Spring, on the western edge of Red Lake (dry); Breon, near Hackberry in the east central part of the county; Black Rock Spring, in the extreme northwestern corner of the county; Camp Beale Springs, about four miles northwest of Kingman; Cave Spring, along Hurricane Cliffs in the north central section of the county; Clack, in the Cerbat Mountains northwest of Kingman; Coyote Hole, in the southern fringes of the Cerbat Mountains; Cyclopic, north of Kingman; Dinoah, at the head of Detrital Valley; El Dorado Mill, on the Colorado River opposite the mouth of El Dorado Canyon (California); Fort Rock, about 40 miles north of Kingman.

Layne City, northwest of Kingman; Hot Spring, on the Colorado River below Boulder Dam; Mountain Spring, in the north central part of the county; Music Mountain, about 25 miles north of Hackberry; New London, northwest of Kingman; New Virginia, on the Big Sandy River in the southeastern corner of the county; Peacock Spring, in the area of Truxton; Pyramid, also known as Sheeptrail, near Kingman; Rawhide; Sandy, near Kingman; Spencer's Ranch, in the east central section of the county; Salt Spring, in the northern reaches of the Black Mountains; Sweeney, on the Colorado River about opposite Needles, California; Wolf Spring, in the extreme northeastern corner of county.

Navajo County—Possible ghost towns include Franklin Spring, southeast of Snowflake; Hardy, on the Santa Fe Railroad east of Winslow; Jara Spring, on Leroux Wash in the east central part of county; Pueblo Tecalote, in the east central part of county.

Pima County—The silver and lead mining camp of Total Wreck was located in the Empire Mountains about 30 miles southeast of Tucson. Its peak population reached about 200 and it had several commercial buildings and dwellings. The camp died when the mine supporting it closed. Little remains at the site.

Pima County—Inquire in Tucson (Interstate 10-19) for directions to the ghost town of Twin Buttes, located in the Sierrita Mountains about 23 miles to the south, where legend has it the Spaniards mined copper, silver and gold.

When the Morgan Mine was found in the 1880's, the town of Morgan Camp grew up around it. Its people drifted away when the panic of 1893 hit the nation and the town became a complete ghost. Some years later those buildings worth the effort were moved three miles to the north to become part of the town of Twin Buttes. Only a few rotting timbers mark the site of Morgan Camp today.

Twin Buttes had a post office, railroad station, hotel, several stores, two schools, and a number of saloons and poolhalls. The town was doomed by the stock market crash of 1929, and the post office closed about a year later. When the railroad was abandoned, vandals carried away everything that could be moved. Today a few battered buildings are all that remain. These stand on private property and visitors should be aware that there are several open shafts and unguarded cave-ins in the area.

Pima County—The little Southern Pacific Railroad stop of Pantano, once an important station, is located 21 miles southeast of Tucson. Trains no longer stop here and all that remains are the old station house and the crumbling water tank.

Pima County—Inquire in Tucson (Interstate 10-19) for directions to the site of San Jose del Tucson Mission, at the edge of town. The adobe remains are no longer visible and there are very few signs of the original buildings. About a mile from here are the stone foundations of an old mill along the side of Sentinel Peak. At the base of the peak is the original site of Stjukshon, the Indian village that eventually became Tucson.

Pima County—Inquire in Sells (State 86) for directions to the ghost town of Quijotoa, located on the slope of Ben Nevis Mountain. It is said that the Spanish took ore out of the Quijotoa region as early as 1774. The American town started with the discovery of copper in 1879. The community covered a half square mile and boasted several stores, a post office, telegraph station, a newspaper and daily stage service. The copper ore proved to be shallow and the town was practically abandoned by 1885, its buildings now reduced to crumbling walls.

Somewhere to the west of Santa Rosa Wash (paralleled by State 93), and on the slopes of the Brownell Mountains west of the ghost town of Quijotoa is rumored to be a cache of hundreds of weapons. Traditionally, the Papago Indians cached their weapons near the positions of potential enemies. The site is on the Papago Indian Reservation, and permission to search must be secured from the tribal council headquarters in Sells.

Pima County—The ghost town of Greaterville lies on the southeastern slopes of the Santa Rita Mountains about 35 miles southeast of Tucson. It can be reached to the west of State 83, but it is suggested that directions and inquiries as to road conditions be secured in Sonoita (State 83). Gold was discovered here in 1873 and miners and prospectors were soon flocking to the area. New strikes were made daily, and in 1875 a town named Santa Rita was found on Greater Creek, attracting those who had established nearby camps—Musick's Camp on Smith Creek, Harshaw's Camp on Mac Creek, and others. In 1879 the town acquired a post office and the name was changed to Greaterville. The supply of yellow ore seemed inexhaustible and the town grew by leaps and bounds. But the boom gradually died as the ore played out, and by 1963 Greaterville was the home of only three or four families. A few overlooked nuggets of gold are still occasionally found here.

TREASURE GUIDE

Pima County—The ruins of Fort Lowell are located on Fort Lowell Road four miles east of Tucson. This was one of the key outposts in the long war carried on by the early settlers against the Apaches. In 1873 Camp Lowell was moved here from Tucson. Abandoned in 1891, soon after the Apache warfare had ended, the buildings immediately began to deteriorate at the hands of desert winds and vandals. The City of Tucson acquired the eastern part of the fort grounds and converted it into a park, reconstructing about a third of the buildings. The remainder, located on private lands, are half weathered away and overgrown with desert verdure.

Pima County—The silver mining camp of Olive was located about 17 miles south of Tucson and was active until about 1885. It was never much of a camp in size, and absolutely nothing remains but the site.

Pima County—Inquire in Sonoita (State 82-83) for directions to what is left of the old copper mining town of Rosemont, located about 12 miles to the north. After the closing of the nearby mines and smelter that supported the town, it rapidly faded.

Pima County—Inquire in Marana (Interstate 10) for directions to the site of the original town of Silverbell, 24 miles to the west and near the present town of Silver Bell. Once one of the most important copper mining towns in Arizona, Silverbell had its up and downs as copper prices rose and fell. When the new town of Silver Bell was founded in 1948, old Silverbell died. All traces of the town have disappeared.

Pima County—Inquire in the near ghost town of Quijotoa (State 86) for directions to the site of Allen, on the slopes of Ben Nevis Mountain to the southwest. The camp consisted largely of a small hotel, a few houses and a store or two. Nothing remains of it today.

Pima County—Only a few concrete foundations and ruins mark the site of Clarkson, a copper mining town once boasting a population of 2,000 and 60 or more business establishments. Located one mile east of Ajo (State 85), the town was almost destroyed by a fire in 1931 and never rebuilt.

Pima County—Inquire in Ajo (State 85) for directions to the site of the old silver mining camp of Gunsight, about 16 miles to the southeast. Traces of old foundations are all that remain.

Pima County—About 300 people once resided in the old copper mining camp of Helvetia located in the foothills of the Santa Rita Mountains about 30 miles southeast of Tucson. The closing of the mines in 1931 spelled doom

120

for the camp and its people moved away. The ruins of some adobe and wooden buildings are all that remain.

Pima County—The copper mining camp of Mineral Hill was located about 16 miles south of Tucson. Comprised largely of Mexican miners and laborers, the camp never attained more than 150 population, and was completely abandoned by 1917. Nothing remains at the site.

Pima County—Possible ghost towns include Cababai (100), at the northern edge of the Quijotoa Mountains; Cholla, on the eastern fringes of the Quijotoa Mountains; Cienega, on the Southern Pacific Railroad southeast of Tucson; Apache Pass; Casa Blanca; Empire; Desert, on the Southern Pacific Railroad northwest of Marana; Fremont, near the Mexican border in the southwestern corner of the county; El Paso, near the Mexican border at the southern edge of Altar Valley; Line City; Maxey; Pelton; Las Playas, near the Mexican border in the extreme southwestern corner of the county; Logan City; Providence Wells, in the southern reaches of Altar Vally; Punza del Agua, on the Santa Cruz River south of Tucson.

Pinal County—The famous Silver King Mine supported the town of Pinal, located three miles southwest of Superior (US 60). Originally known as Picket Post, the town grew rapidly to a population of several hundred people. It gradually died with the diminishing quantity of ore and a decline in the price of silver. Hardly anything remains today except dump heaps.

Pinal County—Some abandoned buildings are all that mark the site of the old mining camp of Reymart, located about 11 miles southwest of Superior (US 60).

Pinal County—Inquire in Red Rock (Interstate 10) for directions to the abandoned site of Sasco, once the smelter town for the famed Silver Bell Mine. Having a population of about 800 at its peak, the town died when the smelters closed. Ruins of some stone buildings, foundations and scattered debris are all that remain.

Pinal County—Inquire in Oracle (State 77) for directions to the site of the old mining camp of American Flag, about five miles to the southeast. Nothing remains at the site. Do not confuse this with another American Flag ghost town in Mohave County.

Pinal County—Inquire in Florence (US 80-89) for directions to the site of Cochran, about 15 miles to the east. Once a copper mining and railroad town of considerable importance, it has now all but disappeared.

121

Pinal County—Inquire in Mammoth (State 77) for directions to the site of Copper Creek, in the Galiuro Mountains about 10 miles to the east. All that remains of this once thriving camp are foundations and scattered ruins.

Pinal County—Inquire in Superior (US 60) for directions to the site of the old milling town of DeNoon, located about 13 miles southwest. The short-lived camp attained a population of about 150 before it folded up. Only the site remains today.

Pinal County—Inquire in Apache Junction (US 80-89) for directions to the ruins of Goldfield, about six miles to the northeast. Located on the eastern slopes of the Superstition Mountains, the camp died when the mines closed after a year of operation. Only a few foundations indicate the site.

Pinal County—Picacho Pass is on Interstate 10 about five miles north of Tucson. Here, in 1862, occurred the only Civil War engagement to take place on Arizona soil. It involved no more than 30 men, but some relics are found in the area.

Pinal County—Inquire in Mammoth (State 77) for directions to the site of old Camp Grant, on Arivaipa Canyon about 10 miles to the north. This was the scene of the controversial Camp Grant Massacre. Nothing remains but piles of crumbled adobe to mark the site of the deserted post, and this is almost hidden in a forest of giant cholla cactus. Many relics have been recovered here.

Pinal County—Inquire in Kearny (State 177) for directions to the site of Ray. Kearny was started by former residents of Ray when they abandoned their town. Nearby is the Southern Pacific Railroad station of Ray Junction, which was formerly called Kelvin, a small mining community in the Ray district. A few people still live here, but it is a mere shadow of its former self.

Pinal County—Inquire in Superior (US 60) for directions to the remains of Silver King, once a famous silver mining town. Only the wrecks of a deserted building or two remain of this town which once had a population of 900 and flourished until the price of silver dropped in 1882.

Pinal County—Inquire in Mammoth (State 77) for directions to the site of Tiger, once an important milling town with a population of about 1,800. Located about four miles west of Mammoth, it has completely dis-

ARIZONA

appeared. Map Code 8 E-4

Pinal County—Inquire in Superior (US 60) for directions to the site of Troy, about 15 miles to the southwest. Nothing at all remains of this copper mining camp that once had a population of about 200.

Pinal County—Inquire in Casa Grande (State 93) for directions to the site of Vekol, a silver mining camp of about 170 population at its peak. About all that remains are the ruins of a mill, some adobe buildings and old rock foundations.

Pinal County—The ghost town of Adamsville, sometimes called Sanford, is located about five miles down the Gila River from Florence (US 80-89). "Its houses are empty and going to ruin; its streets are silent and deserted; the coyote and Gila monster gambol undisturbed through its abandoned stores and lonely gin mills," reported the Prescott *Democrat* in 1881. Adamsville, or Sanford, was a thriving town before Florence came into existence, and it had a history of blood and violence as sanguinary as any place in Arizona Territory. When Florence was established, Adamsville declined and today nothing is left to tell of its former greatness. A political grudge was responsible for Adamsville's name being changed to Sanford, but as long as people lived there it was known as Adamsville to them.

Pinal County—Possible ghost towns include Butte (150); Copperopolis; Desert (10); Dudleyville (60), on the San Pedro River south of Winkelman; Golden Eagle (26); Hastings (60); Manlyville (50); Mesaville (50), on the San Pedro River south of Winkelman; Peach Ranch (25); Riverside (50).

Santa Cruz County—Inquire in Nogales (Interstate 19) for directions to the twin ghost towns of Duquesne and Washington Camp, located almost on the Mexican border to the east. Once the mining centers for the Washington Camp smelters, both towns are now deserted except for a handful of people who still hang on. With a peak population of 1,000, only the ruins of the fine homes of mining officials still stand.

Santa Cruz County—Inquire in Patagonia (State 82) for directions to the ghost town of Mowry, about 14 miles distant. Many sturdy adobe buildings mark the site of the Mowry Mine, one of the earliest in Arizona. It was known to the Jesuits, and worked by Mexicans in the 1850's. About $5,000,000 was taken out by Americans when they acquired it. Of the 17 men buried in the Mowry Mine Cemetery, 15 were the victims of violence.

Santa Cruz County—Inquire at Tumacacori National Monument headquarters (US 89) for directions to the ruins of Guevavi Mission, to the west of the Santa Cruz River not very far away. Once a splendid example of Spanish colonial architecture, it is now nothing but crumbling walls and trash-filled yards that have been thoroughly ransacked by relic seekers and treasure hunters. Founded in 1692 by Father Kino, it was the first church erected by Europeans in what is now southern Arizona.

Santa Cruz County—Inquire at Tumacacori National Monument head-quarters (US 89) for directions to the ghost town of Calabasas. Once a turbulent boom town, it boasted having 16 saloons, several gambling halls, two dancehalls, two Chinese gambling halls, an opium den, stores, lodging houses and other commercial establishments. In its wild days it was known as "Hell's Hollow."

As early as 1777, mines in the vinicity were worked by Spaniards. For a period it was a Mexican military post. In 1856 it was occupied by U. S. Dragoons, and in 1865 an American settlement was established when it was named Calabasas. In 1864 Fort Mason was established here, and the wealth of the nearby mines caused a tremendous boom. The Santa Rita Hotel built here was called the finest between St. Louis and San Francisco.

When the mines collapsed in 1893, people in this wild, riotous town began to drift away. By 1900 Calabasas had a population of only 100, mostly Mexicans. In 1913 the post office closed and a court verdict evicted the settlers. Stores closed and Calabasas was dead. In recent years the old buildings have been razed and the soil cleared for farming. Only a marker indicates the site.

Santa Cruz County—Inquire in Patagonia (State 82) for directions to Harshaw, about 10 miles to the southeast. With a population of about 200 at its peak, Harshaw still has a few permanent residents, mostly Mexicans who know the town as Durazno. A combination of fire, flood and the closing of the nearby mines spelled the town's doom. Only a few of the old commercial buildings remain.

Santa Cruz County—The little settlement of Lochiel, on the Mexican border about 23 miles east of Nogales, still has a small population, but nothing like it had when it was a bustling mining town. It is believed that the town was also called La Noria and Luttrell, or that two small communities with these names once existed nearby, now completely obliterated.

Santa Cruz County—Inquire in Nogales (Interstate 19) for directions to the site of Old Glory, about 24 miles to the northwest. The peak population of this old mining camp never reached more than about 50. Nothing at all remains of it today.

ARIZONA

Santa Cruz County—The almost extinct old mining town of Ruby will be found on State 289 about 36 miles northwest of Nogales, and a few miles from the Mexican border. A once lively mining camp known as Montant Camp, it is located in the Oro Blanco Mountains from which the wealth first came to make the town possible. With the depletion of the ores, the town slowly died, but was revived in 1927 and grew into a town of 2,000 population when a pipeline brought in the necessary water for deep drilling. From 1934 to 1941 the Montana Mine was Arizona's largest producer of lead-zinc. By 1941 the ores were exhausted again and Ruby slowly became a ghost town at the mercy of vandals. Roofs have caved in on the old buildings and only a few are standing in fair condition. Until a few years ago, at least, a caretaker was in charge of the old mining camp, and you will have to secure permission to do any searching.

Santa Cruz County—The old town of Oro Blanco, now deserted, was located near the present settlement of Oro Blanco, about 25 miles northwest of Nogales. The town had a peak population of 225, but nothing remains of it today.

Santa Cruz County—Inquire in Patagonia (State 82) for directions to the site of Salero, nearby. The first mines here were worked by Mexicans. Americans eventually took over the mines, but when the ores were depleted, the town faded. Very little remains today.

Santa Cruz County—Possible ghost towns include Crittenden (65), probably on an abandoned section of the Southern Pacific Railroad in the area of Patagonia; Isaacson, on the Mexican border in the area of Nogales—it may be a part of Nogales; Pajarito, west of the Santa Cruz River in the southwestern corner of the county.

Yavapai County—Inquire in Cordes (State 69) for directions to Baby Canyon Ruins on the south bank of the Agua Fria River in Baby Canyon. The major site consists of 100 rooms below the escarpment of the canyon rim and overlooks eight minor sites. This ancient city is swiftly crumbling to dust. Only partial excavation has been made.

Yavapai County—In 1864, a fight between a party of Arizona pioneers and Apache Indians took place about 20 miles southeast of Prescott, on the flat valley of Turkey Creek near its junction with Tuscumbia Creek. Only one white man died later of his wounds, but 13 Indians were killed. Relics of the fight were being picked up in a widely scattered area around the site many years later.

Yavapai County—The practically extinct town of Bumble Bee still appears on maps just to the west of Interstate 16 about 67 miles north of

Phoenix. The entire town of Bumble Bee is today owned by one man who is rejuvenating it as a sort of living museum to the Old West. The town is one of the oldest settlements in northern Arizona, being first settled by a small detachment of U. S. soldiers as an outpost against hostile Indians. First called Snyder's Station, it received its present name about 1870. Upon three separate occasions the town has moved to remain on the highway. Although you won't be able to do any searching in Bumble Bee without permission of its owner, the area immediately surrounding it has proved to be rich in relics.

Yavapai County—Inquire in Prescott (US 89) for directions to the site of Bueno, about 22 miles to the south. Once an active mining center with a population of about 300, the camp declined with the depletion of the Bully Bueno gold ledge in about 1900. Absolutely nothing remains today at the site.

Yavapai County—Inquire in Prescott (US 89) for directions to the site of Big Bug, about 12 miles southeast. Very little remains of this old camp that once had a population of 125. It once had several stores and a smelter where more than $1,000,000 worth of gold was processed.

Yavapai County—Inquire in Prescott (US 89) for directions to the site of Catoctin, an old mining camp located on Upper Hassayampa Creek about 16 miles to the southeast. Catering to the Catoctin and Climax gold mines, the town never attained a population of more than about 25. Only the site remains today.

Yavapai County—Inquire in Prescott (US 89) for directions to the town of Cherry, not quite a ghost today but only a shadow of its boom days when it had a population of about 400 and more than 40 mines were producing in the area. Some abandoned buildings of its early days still stand.

Yavapai County—Inquire in Prescott (US 89) for directions to the site of the original Camp Whipple, about 20 miles to the north in Little Chino Valley. In 1863 it was occupied by two companies of California Volunteers. In the following year it was moved to its present site near Prescott. Many relics have been found in the area.

Yavapai County—The ruins of Kirkland Creek Fortress is in the vicinity where US 89 crosses Kirkland Creek between Prescott and Peeples Valley. This prehistoric fort, situated on a 4,000-foot plateau overlooking Kirkland Valley to the north, is in a surprisingly good state of preservation. The ruins consist largely of two walls.

ARIZONA

Yavapai County—Inquire in Prescott (US 89) for directions to the town of Walker, located on an unnumbered road. This was once a noted mining camp on Lynx Creek, and was Arizona's richest placer gold mining field during the early days. Gold was discovered here in 1863 by a man named Miller, but the placers were developed by Capt. Joe R. Walker and named for him. Pieces of pure metal worth hundreds of dollars were found in the bedrock. Only butcher knives were needed to pry the gold loose from the rock seams, and it was not unusual to find $5,000 worth of gold under a single boulder. Although the town of Walker is only a shadow of its former self when it had 2,000 population, it is one of the most interesting near ghosts in Arizona. In the gulches and ravines around it were several crowded camps, now completely disappeared.

Yavapai County—The site of the mining camp of Senator, once supported by the Senator gold mine, is located about 11 miles south of Prescott. Revived from time to time, the town is now a complete ghost rapidly falling into decay.

Yavapai County—Inquire in Prescott (US 89) for directions to the site of Venezia, located on the slopes of Mt. Union about 20 miles to the south. Nothing but ruined buildings mark the site of this once important mining center.

Yavapai County—Inquire in Prescott (US 89) for directions to the site of Howells, located about 12 miles to the south. Founded in the 1800's, nothing but ruins remain of this old mining camp and smelter site.

Yavapai County—The site of the old mining camp of Poland is located on Big Bug Creek about nine miles southeast of Prescott. A few summer cottages and homes now occupy the site and very few ruins are left.

Yavapai County—State 49, for its 94-mile stretch from Phoenix to Prescott, is known as the Black Canyon Highway. Black Canyon Hill, 38 miles south of Prescott, was a dangerous one-way grade where stage drivers had to pull into turnouts to pass each other. It was the scene of many stage holdups, and it is suspected that some of the loot secured may still be cached in the area.
The town of Gillette, founded in 1870 as the mill town for the famed Tip Top Mine, was located two miles from here on the banks of the Agua Fria River. By 1878 it was important enough to have a post office, several large stores, saloons, a brewery, brothels, boarding houses, a hotel and other commercial establishments. Only crumbled foundations of these buildings remain today and they are almost concealed by trees.

TREASURE GUIDE

Yavapai County—Inquire in Cordes (State 69) for directions to Crown King, located on an unnumbered road to the southwest. Inquire in Crown King, an old mining town with a few permanent residents, for directions to the site of Bradshaw City, which grew into a booming mining town on the south slope of Wasson Peak, highest point in the Bradshaw Mountains. In 1871 Bradshaw City had a population of 5,000 and supported several stores, restaurants; saloons and other businesses. Nothing exists today except stone foundations and an old cemetery shaded by huge pines and oaks. The site is reached over dim trails and may be difficult to locate without a guide.

Yavapai County—Jerome (US Alternate US 89), with a population of some 500 today, is hardly a ghost town, but it had 5,000 people when it was a booming mining camp. Indians had mined copper here long before the arrival of white men. After the price of copper declined, the population of Jerome gradually decreased, and the death knell came with the closing of the copper mines in 1953. The town hangs precariously on the side of Mingus Mountain, its frame houses a jumble on stilts. Many of them today are deserted and in ruins.

Yavapai County—Inquire in Prescott (US 89) for directions to the site of Oro, also known as Oro Belle, far up in the Bradshaw Mountains on a precipitous slope of Wasson Peak. The little mining town was founded in 1900 and was granted a post office in 1904, but by 1907 it was slipping into oblivion. All that remain are a dozen or so ruined houses, the old bank vault and its battered safe, and the wrecks of a store or two. The elevation is 5,300 feet and the site is almost concealed by cottonwood trees.

Yavapai County—Inquire in Humboldt (State 69) for directions to the site of McCabe, an old mining camp having a population of about 600 at its peak. When the McCabe gold mine closed in 1913, the people gradually left. Only piles of ruins and an old cemetery indicate the site today.

Yavapai County—Richinbar, located about five miles east of Bumble Bee, was once a small camp supported by the Richinbar Mine. Never having more than 50 population, it is now completely deserted and in ruins.

Yavapai County—Inquire in Prescott (US 89) for directions to the site of Placerita, located in Placerita Gulch about 20 miles to the south. Only the ruins of some old buildings and piles of rubble mark the site of this deserted mining camp.

Yavapai County—Inquire in Kirkland (State 71) for possible directions to the site of Zonia, one of the most forgotten ghost towns in Arizona. Located high in the Bradshaw Mountains, the site will probably be difficult to locate without a guide. A very few tumbled down buildings are about all that remain of this old camp which had a peak population of no more than 150. This was copper country and many open shafts make it a dangerous region to explore. Perhaps few people other than natives in the area have ever seen the remains of Zonia.

Yavapai County—Inquire in Congress (US 89) for directions to Rich Hill, visible in the distance to the east. Every foot of soil on the hill was overturned in the mad search for gold after it was discovered by Mexicans rounding up straying horses. It is estimated that within the first month of mining here, $250,000 worth of gold was picked up on the surface. The tumbled walls of cabins built atop the hill by miners are all that remain of the camp.

At the foot of the east side of Rich Hill once stood the little settlement of Weaver, a Mexican adobe town with a history of blood and thunder so violently filled with stage holdups, robberies, murders and general lawlessness that its stain cannot be wiped away by the passing of time. The town actually died as the result of a sensational murder, that of William Segna. People moved away to Congress in fear of their lives. With the exception of a few wrecked houses, the town has completely disappeared.

The Mexican settlement of Weaver should not be confused with an American settlement of the same name farther up the mountain.

Yavapai County—Inquire in Congress (US 89) for directions to Rich of Stanton, also known as Antelope Station, located at the base of Rich Hill and on Antelope Creek. The camp once had a population of about 200, but all that remains are the ruins of a few buildings.

Yavapai County—Inquire in Mayer (State 69) for directions to the remains of the copper mining camp of Stoddard, located about five miles to the east. Attaining a population of about 200 in 1925, the slump in copper prices soon brought an end to the town. Only some ruined buildings remain today.

Yavapai County—Inquire in Mayer (State 69) for directions to the small community of Bluebell, now almost abandoned. Located in the foothills of the Bradshaw Mountains, and supported by the famous Blue Bell Mine, it was once one of the most important copper mining camps in the area. Falling copper prices brought about its demise.

Yavapai County—Inquire in Mayer (State 69) for directions to the site of Alexandra, an old mining camp built up around the Peck Mine in Peck

Canyon. The town flourished, growing into a place of about 100 commercial establishments before the mine became involved in litigations and was forced to close. Its people slowly drifted away until nothing remains at the site today.

Yavapai County—Inquire in Mayer (State 69) for instructions to reach the near ghost town of Cleator, once a prominent mining center. Like most of the many towns in this area depending upon mining activity, the town all but ceased to exist when the mines closed down.

Yavapai County—Inquire in Wickenburg (US 60-89) for directions to the ghost town of Columbia, located on Humbug Creek about 25 miles to the west. Nothing at all remains of this mining camp that once had a population of 100 or more.

Yavapai County—Inquire in Wickenburg (US 60-89) for directions to the near ghost town of Constellation, located on an unnumbered graded road about 11 miles to the northeast. Once an important mining camp of about 300 people, it is still in a productive copper and silver mining area, but only a few people live here today and most of the old town is in ruins.

Yavapai County—The town of Congress is located on US 89 about 17 miles north of Wickenburg. The original town of Congress was located about three miles south of the present town, and was once a mining community of about 500 people and several commercial establishments. When the railroad built through three miles to the north, a new town called Congress Junction (the "Junction" was later dropped) sprang up. The original town gradually died and only its ruins are still visible.

Yavapai County—Inquire in Rock Springs (State 69) for directions to the ruins of Tip Top, a deserted silver mining camp. Once an active camp, Tip Top was dead by 1895, victim of the drop in the price of silver. Nothing but the rubble-covered site remains.

Yavapai County—Ask in Humboldt (State 69) for directions to the site of Chaparral, about four miles to the west. This mining camp flourished in the 1890's, attaining a top population of about 100. People gradually moved away to the nearby town of McCabe (now almost a ghost) until Chaparral disappeared completely. Nothing at all remains of it.

Yavapai County—Between US 89 and the Santa Fe Railroad tracks about 30 miles south of Ashfork, are the Del Rio Ruins. The remains of these prehistoric dwellings have been excavated, but artifacts are still found in the area. The site is near the small town of Drake (US 89).

ARIZONA

Yavapai County—Possible ghost towns include Juniper, at the western edge of Black Mountain; Whitmore, in the northwestern corner of the county; Meesville, on the western edge of the Bradshaw Mountains; Minnehaha, on the northwestern slopes of the Bradshaw Mountains; Hassayampa, southwest of Prescott.

Yuma County—Inquire in Parker (State 95) for directions to the site of Swansea, about 30 miles east. The mining camp, originally known as Signal, reached a peak population of about 800 and had several stores and saloons. It ceased to exist in about 1924 when the mines supporting it closed. Only a few crumbling buildings indicate the site.

Yuma County—Inquire in Parker (State 95) for directions to the ghost town of Planet, located on the Bill Williams River about 15 miles to the northeast. It became a ghost about 1917 when the copper mines supporting it closed down. Nothing at all remains.

Yuma County—Inquire in Salome (US 60) for directions to the old mining camp of Harrisburg, now a ghost. In a small cemetery here are the remains of the members of a wagon train party killed by Indians as they were on their way to California in 1849. The bleached bones of the party were found on the desert months later.

Yuma County—The site of old Fort Tyson is located at the edge of Quartzsite (US 60). Never a regular army post, the fort was built in 1856 by settlers as protection against marauding Mojave Indians.

Yuma County—The ghost town of La Paz, of which nothing at all remains, was located about 18 miles from Quartzsite (US 60) where inquiries should be made. The seat of Yuma County until 1870, gold was discovered here in 1862, and the town grew to a population of some 6,000 people, becoming the most important town in Arizona. In a period of seven years, millions were taken from its placers. When they played out, the town quickly vanished. Perhaps La Paz attained a greater population than any other ghost town in Arizona, and perhaps its site is as barren as any.

Yuma County—Although Ehrenberg still appears on maps (US 60 at the Colorado River), it is essentially a ghost town of fast crumbling adobe walls. In 1871 it had a population of about 500 and was an important shipping point for Prescott, La Paz and other mining districts.

Yuma County—Inquire in Yuma (US 80) for directions to the site of Gila City, on the Gila River about 20 miles to the east. In 1858 rich gold placers were discovered here and the camp established here mushroomed into a turbulent town of 1,200 people. A disastrous flood hit the town in 1862 and two years later it was deserted. Only the wrecks of a few chimneys remain.

Yuma County—Inquire in Yuma (US 80) for directions to the ruins of Hacienda de San Ysidro, known also as Redondo Ruins. This was once the greatest ranch in what is now the State of Arizona, serving also as a supply point for La Paz and the gold camps along the Colorado River. The ranch, comprised largely of appropriated public lands, was broken up when U. S. land laws were made applicable to territorial possessions. When its owner walked away in disgust, rumors spread that he had left a buried fortune behind and an influx of treasure hunters dug so many holes in the main building that its walls collapsed for lack of support.

Yuma County—Castle Dome Landing was a shipping point on the Colorado River for the mines in the Castle Dome Mountains. It was located about 30 miles north of Yuma and never acquired more than 50 or so permanent residents. Today the site is all or partially covered by the waters backed up by the Imperial Dam.

Yuma County—Inquire in Yuma (US 80) for directions to the site of the old mining camp of Fortuna, located in the southern slopes of the Gila Mountains about 45 miles to the southeast. Nothing at all remains at the site, and visitors should be warned that it is near the famed **Camino del Diablo**, a pioneer trail which traverses one of the most dangerous sections of desert in the Southwest.

Yuma County—Inquire in Yuma (US 80) for directions to the site of Silent, the old mining camp for the Red Cloud Mine, located about 20 miles north and not far east of the Colorado River. Because of a shortage of lumber, most of the dwellings were simple dugouts. A dozen or more frame or adobe buildings comprised the business district, and all are in ruins today. The town died in 1893 with a decline in the price of silver.

Yuma County—Inquire in Yuma (US 80) for directions to the site of Norton's Landing on the Colorado River about 20 miles to the north. This was the smelting plant town for the famous Red Cloud Mine and a shipping center for other mines in the area. It also passed from being in 1893 and nothing remains of it today.

Yuma County—Inquire in Wellton (US 80) for directions to Tinajas Altas Springs, about 30 miles to the south and reached by an unnumbered graveled road. Tinajas Altas (high tanks) are a group of eight natural cavities in the granite rocks that retain water for most of the year—the only water found in a large area. Wheel ruts still visible mark the fearful **Camino del**

ARIZONA

Diablo (Devil's Road), the trail followed by Father Kino on his missionary trip from his headquarters in Sonora to the mouth of the Colorado River. It was so named from the toll of lives it took from travelers, an estimated 3,000 to 4,000 dying along its route from hunger, thirst and fatigue. A great many Spanish relics are still found along its course. Do not attempt to travel in this section of Arizona without being accompanied by a person experienced in the ways of the desert.

Yuma County—The completely vanished town of Clip was located on the Colorado River about 40 miles north of Yuma. Here was located the mill to work the ore of the Silver Clip Mine. At one time it attained a population of 200, but they disappeared when the mine's activity declined. Nothing at all remains of it.

Yuma County—Inquire in Salome (US 60) for directions to the ghost town of Harqua Hala, in the Harquahala Mountains about 12 miles to the south. The boom town grew up here with the discovery of gold, but dissolved into oblivion when the ore was exhausted. Only a scattering of ruined buildings remain.

Yuma County—Inquire in Quartzsite (US 60-95) for directions to the ghost town site of Kofa, about 14 miles to the southwest. This was the camp for the famous King of Arizona gold mine in the Kofa Mountains. The town was virtually abandoned when the mines in the area shut down in 1919, and all that remains today are scattered ruins and an old cemetery.

Yuma County—The site of Olive City is located near the Colorado River about 15 miles south of the near ghost town of Ehrenberg (US 60), where inquiries should be made. Sometimes known as Bradshaw after the man who operated a ferry here, the town never attained a population of more than 20 or so people. There were several business establishments, but absolutely nothing is left of them today.

Yuma County—Inquire in Quartzsite (US 60-95) for directions to the site of Polaris, the old mining camp for the Golden Star Mining Company. Gold was discovered here in the 1890's, but was worked out by 1911 when the camp ceased to exist. Nothing but rubble remains to mark the site.

Yuma County—Possible ghost towns include Hawk Spring, on the western slopes of the Plomosa Mountains; Plomosa, on the eastern slopes of the Plomosa Mountains; Granite Water, on the western slopes of the Granite Wash Mountains; Mineral City, on or near the Colorado River south of Ehrenberg; Mammoth Spring, at the southern end of the Castle Dome Moun-

133

tains; Adonde, an old railroad station on the Southern Pacific east of Yuma; Corral, at the southern tip of the Sierra Pinta Range; Albino, near the Mexican border in the southwestern corner of the county.

THE END